Published in 2011 by Stewart, Tabori & Chang
An imprint of ABRAMS

Text copyright © 2011 Kelly Wilkinson
Photographs copyright © 2011
Thayer Allyson Gowdy

Library of Congress Cataloging-in-Publication
Data
Wilkinson, Kelly.
Weekend handmade : more than 40 projects
and ideas for inspired crafting / Kelly Wilkinson ;
photographs by Thayer Allyson Gowdy.
       p. cm.
"A Melanie Falick book."
ISBN 978-1-58479-940-5 (alk. paper)
1. Handicraft. I. Title.
TT145.W55 2011
745.5--dc22   2010046871

Editor: Melanie Falick
Designer: onethread
Production Manager: Tina Cameron

The text of this book was composed in
Berthold Akzidenz Grotesk, Chronicle Text,
Helvetica Neue, and hand-drawn letterforms.

Printed and bound in China
10 9 8 7 6 5 4 3 2 1

Stewart, Tabori & Chang books are available
at special discounts when purchased in quantity
for premiums and promotions as well as
fundraising or educational use. Special editions
can also be created to specification. For details,
contact specialsales@abramsbooks.com or the
address below.

ABRAMS
THE ART OF BOOKS SINCE 1949

115 West 18th Street
New York, NY 10011
www.abramsbooks.com

Weekend Handmade

MORE THAN
40 PROJECTS + IDEAS
FOR INSPIRED CRAFTING

KELLY WILKINSON

PHOTOGRAPHS BY THAYER ALLYSON GOWDY
PHOTOSTYLING BY KAREN SCHAUPETER

STC CRAFT | A MELANIE FALICK BOOK | STEWART, TABORI & CHANG | NEW YORK

contents

introduction

In the midst of a busy week, the promise of the weekend glints in the distance.
During the week, I sometimes feel like I don't own my time. It belongs to work, deadlines, commitments, and to-do lists. While those obligations are necessary parts of a full life, any leftover time during the week can feel a little squeezed. But weekends are different. Projects can slowly unfurl. Ideas that percolate all week can finally take shape when I have time to gather materials, experiment, and create.

Because I thrive alternately on solitude and company, I try to incorporate both into my weekends. A Saturday or Sunday morning may start with a quiet walk, followed by time spent listening to the radio and reading the newspapers. Evenings might be livelier: friends and family around our big dining room table, with food and wine and games.

On my most ideal weekends, there is always time for crafting. When I have a clutch of empty hours or a whole day or two, I can finally indulge my desire to sit down and make something. Of course, there is the deep satisfaction that comes from being immersed in a process and the subsequent rush of accomplishment. But there is also satisfaction when I realize that what I make reveals something deeper. I know the word "values" is overused and has lost a lot of meaning. But I recognize my values in many of my projects. The act of gathering people around a table to eat and talk and laugh is precious to me, and I want my environment to reflect that. So I happily spend time sewing tablecloths, printing napkins, and making centerpieces to enrich that experience.

The same is true of making time to decorate even a simple planter: I love to garden, so every time I open my backdoor to water our back stoop herb garden, seeing that planter brings me a little surge of happiness and pride. The projects I make and the ones I've included in this book reveal what I love and value: items with a story and sense of place; relaxed weekends that include family and friends; a home that is pretty and welcoming.

A lot of this grew out of my childhood. In 1973, my parents moved out of Washington, DC, to a then-small town in Virginia, hemmed in by cornfields. A couple years later, they went whole-hog and bought an old hay barn from a dairy farmer who planned to burn it down. They dismantled the barn and re-assembled it board by board on a new piece of property they bought in the wide-open countryside.

It's a longer story than I have room for here—the money ran out faster than my parents imagined, so my father and then-pregnant mother moved in with two toddlers, without finished plumbing or a front door or kitchen sink. My dad enrolled my mom in a plumbing, wiring, and carpentry course when she was almost seven months pregnant. My older sister and I slept together in a room without windows since there was no glass in any of the frames yet.

Those years were full of challenges for my parents. But, for my sisters and me, the barn was a wildly creative place. It could absorb whatever activity the three of us dreamed up: We rolled back rugs to go roller-skating, drew on concrete floors before carpet went in, and staged elaborate plays on the second-floor walkway. Big Wheels lived side-by-side with carpentry tools and stained-glass supplies. The kitchen table—an old barn door on legs—was where we finished homework while our mother painted, and upstairs my dad kept a table saw and stacks of barn wood to finish the ceiling.

Since the barn was a work-in-progress my entire childhood, I sort of feel like we grew up together—the barn and I—uncovering who we were going to become. In many ways, I have held tight to that love of transformation. As my parents turned an old hay barn into a home, I have always been drawn to taking simple materials and transforming them into projects that feel sophisticated and intimate.

I went on to college, and then for years lurched back and forth between journalism and more traditionally "creative" work. I would work as a reporter in a newsroom for a couple of years, then quit and do something radically different, and then return again to journalism. Along the way, I stitched and sold a line of aprons and worked in a jewelry studio and at a knitting design company.

Finally, I think I have found my niche. I work in public radio as a reporter, and I also design craft projects for magazines, newspapers, and websites. In 2008, I started a blog called Make Grow Gather, and began work on what would ultimately become this book. In retrospect, the detours that I once considered wildly incongruous now make sense within this integrated life of journalism and crafting.

Today I live in a city apartment, where I try to reconcile the very different worlds of my dreamy rural childhood and urban adulthood. Sometimes, I'm conflicted and want to flee to the country full-time. I chalk this up to being equal parts Laura Ingalls and Holly Golightly. But San Francisco lets me indulge that whole range of personality. I can hop a train downtown to catch a movie or meet a friend for a cocktail, but I can also grow vegetables in my backyard or hike along a trail that's thick with blackberries in the summer.

The projects in this book are born out of all these interests, and divided into sections called Make, Grow, and Gather. While all the projects could be categorized as Make, I followed the structure of my blog to inspire projects that fall into three general categories: The Make section offers projects you might make to wear or decorate a home. Projects in the Grow section draw inspiration from gardens, fields, and farmer's markets. And Gather projects can be used to pretty-up casual weekend get-togethers.

Weekend Handmade follows on from two other crafting books, *Weekend Knitting* by Melanie Falick and *Weekend Sewing* by Heather Ross. While each of those books depended upon readers having a certain mastery of a skill, this book is for crafty dabblers like me who enjoy experimenting with different, easy techniques. I'm as inspired wandering the aisles of my local hardware store as I am perusing the stalls at a flea market. I don't consider myself an expert—rather the product of a lifetime spent making things and finding what works best for my projects. Hopefully, the projects here will appeal to experienced crafters looking for creative new ideas, as well as people who don't consider themselves especially skilled but nonetheless feel the tug of wanting to make something beautiful by hand.

For many people, time—or the lack thereof—is a powerful deterrent. I've tried to remove that hurdle with these projects. All of them can be accomplished in the space of a Saturday and Sunday, but many require far less time. So, whether you have a whole weekend or just a few hours to devote to making something, you will find a project to satisfy. Along the way, I hope you will discover what I've found: that the joy of crafting hits twice. First, when you're lost in the process of making something with your hands; and again after you finish a project and it becomes part of the landscape of your life. Pillows, pressed-flower lanterns, or jars of orange marmalade blazing out from a kitchen shelf—they all serve as beautiful reminders of time you took to slow down, savor, and enjoy.

Kelly

make

chapter 1

Winter Blossoms Cowl

Felting is an addictive alchemy that isn't hard to master. This project, for example, begins as a pile of beat-up old wool sweaters and ends as a casual, graceful cowl. The finished piece is cozy, elegant, and organic all at the same time, perfect for weekend walks and other outdoor activities.

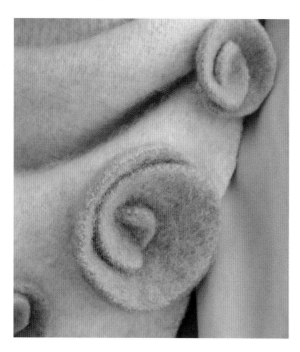

FINISHED DIMENSIONS

9" (23 cm) wide x 15" (38 cm) long

MATERIALS

Felted sweaters (see note below)
   or wool felt in 2–3 colors for flower
   embellishments
½ yard (½ meter) fleece or a felted
   sweater for cowl
Thread to match fabrics
Chalk or chalk pencil
Drinking glass or other circular
   objects (optional)
Fabric scissors
Straight pins
Sewing needle
Clear acrylic grid ruler
Sewing machine
Safety pins

NOTE: Felting sweaters is easy, but requires advance planning, because it takes time for them to dry. Look for solid color, 100% wool sweaters in vintage or thrift stores. Set a washing machine to the hottest setting and add the sweaters—no need to add detergent. Wash the sweaters, checking them after the agitation cycle to see if they have felted. You'll know they're done when you can't see the stitches anymore and the wool has shrunk into a thick, dense material. If this doesn't happen on the first cycle, repeat the agitation cycle until the sweaters have felted. Spin the sweaters to remove excess water, and then lay them flat on towels to dry.

Make Flower Embellishments

1. Using a chalk pencil, draw five to seven circles varying between 1½″ (4 cm) and 3″ (7.5 cm) in diameter onto felted sweaters or wool felt by tracing the outline of a drinking glass or other circular object. Cut out the circles, cutting just inside the marked lines, or if you prefer, cut out circles freehand.

2. Holding a felted circle in one hand, begin cutting into the circle at the outside edge, making a spiraling cut by curving in toward the center and ending at the center. If this process leaves the end with a sharp tail, trim off about ½″ (1.5 cm) at the end of the spiral to remove the sharp tail.

3. Starting at the center of the spiral, coil the fabric so the layers overlap and stack around the center piece to create a flower shape. After you try a few, you may want to vary the symmetry of your flowers, stacking some toward the right or left. Pin the layers in place.

4. Thread a needle with a double-length of thread and knot the ends together. Starting at the center of flower, on the wrong side, insert the needle from back to front, take a small stitch to the back, and repeat several times to tack the layers into place. End with the needle on the wrong side. Knot the thread and trim off the excess.

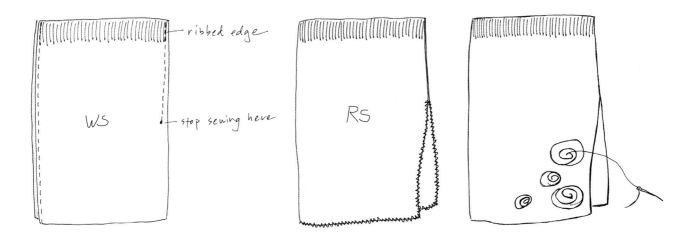

Make Cowl (steps 2–7): Pin, then sew together the two pieces of felt or fleece, right sides facing. Then turn cowl right side out and zigzag stitch along raw edges. Finally, tack the flowers into place.

5. Re-thread the needle in the same manner as before. On the wrong side of the coil, tack the layers together along the length of the spiral, working from the outer edge toward the center, keeping the stitches on the back side. When you reach the center, pass the needle back and forth on the back side of the flower. Knot the thread and trim the thread tails.

6. Repeat steps 2–5 to make additional flowers.

Make Cowl

1. Lay out the felted sweater or fold a piece of fleece in half and cut out two rectangles measuring 10″ x 15″ (25 x 38 cm). I like to place one short edge of each rectangle along the ribbed hem of the sweater and use this edge as the upper edge of the cowl.

2. Place the rectangles right sides together and pin along the edges. Make a mark with a chalk pencil on one long side of the rectangles, 8″ (20.5 cm) from the upper edges.

3. Sew the unmarked long side of the cowl, right sides together, using ½″ (1.5 cm) seam allowances and backstitching at the beginning and end.

4. Stitch the remaining long sides together, starting at the top and sewing down to the mark 8″ (20.5 cm) from the top. Backstitch at the beginning and end. Turn right-side out.

5. If you want to add a decorative stitch along the raw edges, stitch around them, using a zigzag stitch, being careful to sew through only one layer of fabric at a time.

6. Arrange the flowers on the cowl as desired and pin in place with safety pins. I like to clump the flowers toward one side of the split, and have them cascade down toward the bottom.

7. Hand-sew each flower in place.

This dramatic headband flatters any hair length (even my short crop). Wear it to a festive weekend party and accessorize with a glass of champagne. Or add some panache to a low-key weekend afternoon.

Feathered Headband

FINISHED DIMENSIONS

Feather pad: 4" (10 cm) wide x 5" (12.5 cm) high

MATERIALS

Plain or fabric-wrapped headband
4–5" (10–12.5 cm) tall feather pad (called a pad when the feathers are already attached to a backing; see Resources)
⅛ yard (⅛ meter) feather trim, or smaller loose feathers, for accent
Decorative button or clip-on earring, with earring back removed (see "Prepare Baubles" in the Bohemian Necklace project on page 28 for instructions)
Clothespin
Felt to match headband
Thread to match felt
Permanent bonding cement or strong glue
Fabric scissors
Large mirror, to check placement of feather pad while wearing headband
Chalk pencil
Double-sided tape
Sewing needle

Make Feather Piece

NOTE: When you buy feather pads, some of the backings can be harder to sew through than others. If you find you have a feather pad that you can't get a needle through, you can always glue the pad and felt together with bonding cement and skip the sewing step.

1. If using feather trim by-the-yard (meter), remove some feathers from the trim. Arrange the loose feathers on top of the feather pad, at the tapered end. Secure in place with bonding cement and let dry.

2. Position a decorative button or clip-on earring front to the base of feathers to conceal the ends. Secure in place with bonding cement and let dry. Use a clothespin to help keep the button or earring in place as it dries.

Assemble Headband

1. If any of the downy fluff on small feathers is visible when you remove the clothespin, trim with scissors.

2. Lay the feather pad on a piece of felt and trace the entire outline onto the felt with a chalk pencil. Cut ½" (1.5 cm) inside the chalk line, so the felt is smaller than the feather pad.

3. Try on the headband in front of a mirror. Position the feather pad in desired position on the side of the headband and temporarily secure with a piece of double-sided tape. Remove headband.

4. Thread a needle with a double-length of thread and knot the ends together.

5. Place the felt on the inside of the headband, so the headband is sandwiched between the felt and the wrong side of the feather pad (see illustration below).

6. Using a whipstitch, sew the edge of the felt to the feather pad, being careful not to push the needle through to the front of the feather pad. When you reach the headband at the top of the feather pad, pass the needle under the felt and headband. Then continue sewing along the other side. Knot the thread at the end and trim the thread tails.

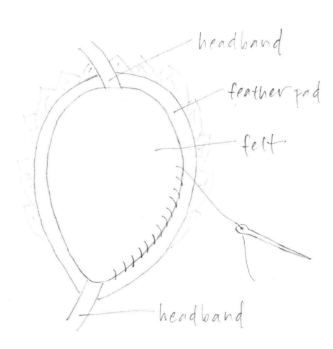

Assemble Headband (Steps 6–7):
Whipstitch the felt to the underside of the feather pad,
sandwiching the headband between the two.

Sunday Morning Pillows

Nothing captures a lazy weekend quite like reading the newspaper in bed or sprawled on the living room floor, in comfy clothes with a big mug of coffee. But for an ideal experience, you need to be propped up comfortably–no craning your neck to read your favorite section. This big pillow solves that problem, and is also an easy way to introduce favorite fabric colors and prints into your decor.

FINISHED DIMENSIONS

Large pillow: 24" x 24" (61 x 61 cm)
Small pillow: 16" x 16" (40.5 x 40.5 cm)

MATERIALS

For large pillow:
1 yard (1 meter) linen for back panels
¾ yard (¾ meter) main print fabric for
     pillow front
¾ yard (¾ meter) contrasting print fabric
     for pillow front
25" (63.5 cm) grosgrain ribbon,
     2" (5 cm) wide
24" (61 cm) square pillow form

For small pillow:
⅝ yard (⅝ meter) linen for front panel
     and backing
⅝ yard (⅝ meter) contrasting print fabric
     for front panel
17" (43 cm) grosgrain ribbon,
     1" (2.5 cm) wide
16" (40.5 cm) square pillow form

For both pillows:
Thread to match fabrics and ribbon
Rotary cutter
Clear acrylic grid ruler
Self-healing cutting mat
Fabric scissors
Straight pins
Sewing machine
Iron and ironing board

Cut Fabric Pieces for Large Pillow

1. For the pillow front, cut one 16" x 25" (40.5 x 63.5 cm) rectangle from the main print fabric and one 10" x 25" (25.5 x 63.5 cm) rectangle from the contrasting print fabric.

2. For the pillow back, cut two 15½" x 25" (39.5 x 63.5 cm) pieces of linen.

Cut Fabric Pieces for Small Pillow

1. For the pillow front, cut one 12" x 17" (30.5 x 43 cm) rectangle from the main print fabric and one 5" x 17" (12.5 x 43 cm) rectangle from the linen fabric.

2. For the pillow back, cut two 12" x 17" (30.5 x 43 cm) pieces of linen.

Join Pillow Front Panels and Hem Pillow Back Pieces

1. Pin the pillow front pieces right sides together along one long edge. Stitch together, using ½" (1.5 cm) seam allowances and backstitching at the beginning and end. Press the seam allowances open.

2. On the right side, position the length of ribbon on top of the seam and pin. Stitch the ribbon in place along each long edge.

3. On each pillow back piece, fold over and press ½" (1.5 cm) to wrong side on one long edge. Fold over ½" (1.5 cm) again, press, and pin in place. Stitch close to the inner fold.

Assemble Pillow

1. Position the pillow back pieces wrong side down on your work surface, overlapping the hemmed edges at the middle so the pieces make a 24" or 16" (61 or 40.5 cm) square. Pin overlap in place to keep it in position.

2. Position the pillow front on top of the pillow back pieces, right sides together. Pin in place around all four sides.

3. Stitch around the pillow squares, using a ½" (1.5 cm) seam allowance and backstitching at the beginning and end.

4. Clip the corners and trim the seam allowances.

5. Turn the pillow case right side out and insert the pillow form.

Bog Tea

My morning routine can be pretty lackluster stuff: I wake up, take the dog for a walk, eat breakfast, and get working. But since I live in San Francisco, even a ho-hum dog walk has the potential to be inspiring if I take time to notice. That's because most of my walks involve climbing to the top of a hill. In San Francisco, the light shifts and changes so often, and the fog filters the light differently all the time, so even a view that I've seen from the same angle on hundreds of dog walks can look remade from one morning to the next.

Often on weekend mornings, my husband and I go together and we take along a glass bottle of hot tea that we've milked and sugared at home. We began this tradition after my husband told me how his mom, as a little girl in rural Ireland, used to bring tea to older family members and neighbors working at a nearby peat bog, cutting and stacking turf to be used to heat their homes. There were no Thermoses back then, so his mom carried the tea in glass milk or whiskey bottles.

We call this little weekend ritual "bog tea." It may be my sentimentality, but I've come to believe that when we carry the tea in a glass container and drink it outside, it has the taste of that long-ago time. So next time you want to cozy up a morning walk, brew a pot of good, strong Irish tea, carry it outside, and drink in the world.

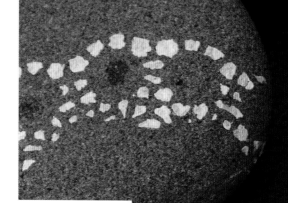

My mother is the best and most inventive "upcycler" I know. Inspired by her, I made this necklace from a combination of flea market baubles and jewelry I inherited from my stylish maternal grandmother. I added a simple buttonhole closure, but you could just as easily leave the ribbons long and simply tie at the back of your neck.

Bohemian Necklace

FINISHED DIMENSIONS:

Necklace: 3½" (9 cm) wide x 24"
(61 cm) long
Central cluster: 3½" (9 cm) high x 4½"
(11.5 cm) wide

MATERIALS

½ yard (½ meter) each of nylon netting in
    four colors
Baubles, such as pins, brooches,
    clip-on earrings, or buttons
    (see note below)
5" x 6" (12.5 x 15 cm) piece muslin
5" x 6" (12.5 x 15 cm) piece wool felt
½ yard (½ meter) ribbon, ⅝" (16 mm) wide
Button, ½" (1.5 cm) diameter to match ribbon
Thread to match grosgrain ribbon
Bullnose pliers
Pin backs (optional)
Permanent bonding cement (optional)
Fabric scissors
Needle
Pencil
Tracing paper for pattern (optional)
Paper scissors (if making a template
    from paper)
Disappearing-ink fabric marker
Straight pins
Button foot for sewing machine or
    fray protector

NOTES: When sourcing baubles for your
necklace, keep in mind that pins will be the
easiest to use because they don't need to
be modified—but make sure the front isn't
too large or heavy, or it might tip forward.
If using earrings or brooches, make sure
they have a flat back so you can easily add a
pin or glue them flat against the necklace.

You can use shank buttons or buttons
with holes. Shank buttons may tip forward;
the thread used to secure two-hole and
four-hole buttons will show on necklace
front, so choose color accordingly.

Prepare Baubles

If using pins or brooches, no preparation is needed, as you can simply pin them in place on the necklace. If you're using clip-on earrings, pry the hinged backing off the earring with a pair of pliers by grasping the hinge with the pliers as close to the base of the earring as possible and moving the clip backing back and forth until it snaps off. If desired, apply a craft pin to the back of the earring using bonding cement and let dry. Alternatively, you can glue items directly to the necklace fabric.

Make Flowers

1. For each flower, cut two pieces of netting 10" (25.5 cm) square and layer the squares (use the same color for both netting squares or use two different colors of netting to add depth). Fold the layered squares in half, then fold in half again two more times to create a small square of folded netting.

2. Thread a needle with thread and knot the thread ends together. Bring the needle up through the center back of the folded netting square. Tack the layers in place several times, finishing with the thread at the back of the square. Don't cut the extra thread yet.

3. To give the flower dimension, fold the layered netting square in half so the knot you just created is in the fold. This creates a pinched effect that will make the flower puffy instead of flat. Tack the layers together several times, 1/4" (6 mm) from the fold.

4. Release the fold, and fold the layered netting square in half in the opposite direction. Again, tack the layers together several times, 1/4" (6 mm) from the fold. Knot at the back and trim the extra thread. Open the square.

5. With fabric scissors, trim the corners of the netting to make a circle about 2½" (6.5 cm) in diameter. Start with the top layers of netting and trim one or two layers at a time, so the layers are staggered and irregular, but gradually get bigger toward the bottom.

6. Repeat steps 1–5 to make another 2½" (6.5 cm) flower and two smaller flowers (trim the netting circle for the small flowers to 1½" (4 cm) in diameter in step 5).

Prepare Necklace Base

1. Place a piece of muslin over the necklace template opposite, trace with a pencil, and cut out just inside the marked lines with fabric scissors. Note: If the muslin is too thick to see the template through the fabric, trace the template onto paper first, cut it out, and then trace the paper template onto the muslin with a disappearing-ink fabric marker. Cut the shape out of muslin, cutting just inside the marked line with fabric scissors.

2. Place the muslin template on top of the wool felt and trace the shape onto the felt with a disappearing-ink fabric marker. Cut out the wool felt, cutting just inside the marked line.

3. Transfer the template markings for the ribbon placement onto the right sides of the muslin and the felt, using a disappearing-ink fabric marker.

Assemble Necklace

1. Position the netting flowers on top of the muslin, and add baubles to some of the flowers' centers; leave others plain. Fill in the gaps between the flowers with the remaining baubles and brooches until you have a pleasing arrangement. Overlap some edges of the flowers so all the elements are tightly clustered on the muslin and no muslin is visible, but be sure not to place anything within ½" (1.5 cm) of the edge to ensure you have enough room to sew the muslin to the felt.

2. When you are satisfied with your arrangement, pin the brooches and items with pin backs in place and secure any elements without pin backs to the arrangement with a needle and thread or glue (sewn items will be more secure than glued items).

3. Carefully turn the necklace upside down so the baubles are face down on the work surface.

4. Place the felt cutout on top of the muslin, aligning markings. The muslin may have pinched a little after sewing the baubles in place. If the edges don't match exactly, that's okay—you can account for this when you sew the pieces together.

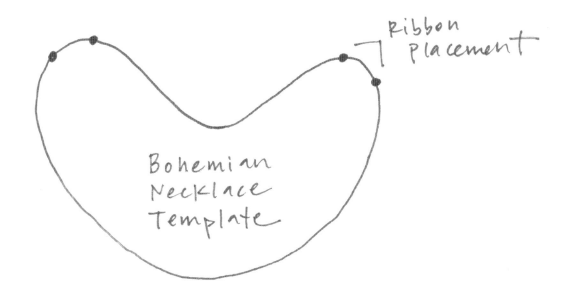

Ribbon Placement

Bohemian Necklace Template

Prepare Necklace Base (Steps 1–3)
Prepare the necklace base by tracing this template onto a piece of muslin and
then use the muslin as a guide for cutting out wool felt.

5. Cut the ½-yard (½-meter) length of ribbon in half. Place the ends of both ribbons so they're sandwiched between the muslin and felt pieces at the marked points. Pin the ribbons in place.

6. Thread a needle with a double length of thread and knot the ends together. Insert the needle from the back to the front where the ribbon is attached to secure the layers together. Hand-stitch the felt and muslin layers together, using a running stitch ¼" (6 mm) from the edge. Securely stitch the ribbon in place.

7. Stand in front of a mirror and hold the necklace around your neck to see where it should hang. Mark the ribbon ends where they should meet at the back of the neck, using a disappearing-ink fabric marker. If you're not adding a button closure, cut ribbon 6" to 8" (15 to 20 cm) beyond the mark to tie around your neck. If you're adding a button closure, cut the ribbon ends 1" (2.5 cm) beyond the marked points.

8. To finish the ends of the ribbon, turn each end ¼" (6 mm) to the wrong side and press in place. Turn another ¼" (6 mm) to the wrong side and press again. Stitch in place with a small running stitch.

9. Add a button closure by sewing a button to the end of one ribbon. Mark the placement of a buttonhole at the end of the other ribbon. Use the button foot on your sewing machine to create a buttonhole. Alternatively, cut a slit in the ribbon at the buttonhole marking, seal the raw edges with fray protector, and bind the cut edges with small overhand stitching.

Prima
Lampshade

This lampshade makeover–built with floaty layers of ballerina netting–adds an air of grace to any tabletop. While I love the diffused light it casts, I might have to surrender it to my niece who, like me, is spellbound by all things ballet.

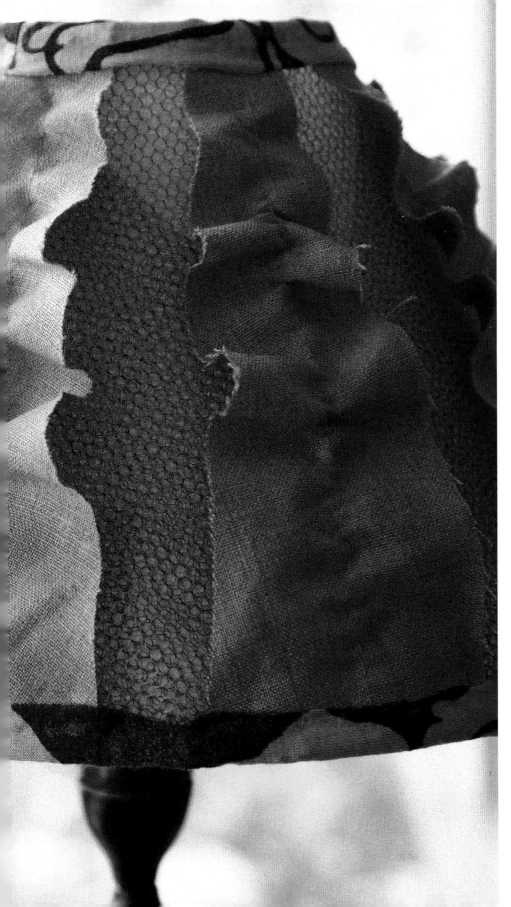

FINISHED DIMENSIONS

4" (10 cm) diameter at top, 10" (25.5 cm) diameter at bottom, and 7" (18 cm) high

MATERIALS

Plain lampshade (drum or tapered, but not accordion style)

½ yard (½ meter) each of three colors of netting (1 ½ yards [1 ½ meters] total) for background

⅜ yard (⅜ meter) linen for ruffled strips

Double-fold bias tape or ribbon, ½" (1.5 cm) or 1" (2.5 cm) wide (amount equal to the circumference of the top and bottom of the shade combined, plus about 4" [10 cm])

Thread to match fabric

Clear acrylic grid ruler

Fabric scissors

Heavy stack of books

Non-flammable spray adhesive

Iron and ironing board

Rotary cutter

Self-healing cutting mat

Sewing machine

Water-soluble fabric glue

Clothespins

Bowl, slightly smaller than the bottom diameter of the shade

NOTE: The fabric yardages given are for a shade of the finished size listed above. If you select a shade with different measurements, the yardage requirements may differ slightly. Bias tape is the easiest trim to use on the edges of the shade, especially for tapered shades, because it will naturally wrap around the curve of the shade. However, ribbon can be used for finishing the edges of drum shades.

Cover Shade with Netting

1. Cut each of the netting fabrics into rough 12″ (30.5 cm) squares.

2. Fold the netting squares in half. The edges don't need to align perfectly—the irregularity will create a layered look. Place books on top of the folded squares to retain their shape.

3. Working outside or in a well-ventilated area, apply a thin coat of spray adhesive to the outside of the lampshade.

4. Position the darkest pieces of folded netting around the lampshade, overlapping as desired until the entire shade is covered. You'll be building the netting up in layers, so don't worry about making the pieces too neat and tidy. The random overlaps add a wispy effect. It is okay to arrange the netting pieces so they hang over the top or bottom of the shade, since the netting will be trimmed even with the edges of the shade before adding the linen strips. Smooth out any wrinkles and let dry.

5. When dry, apply a coat of spray adhesive on top of the netting. Adhere the remaining netting pieces over the previous layer of netting. Be sure to cover the entire surface of the lampshade, including the top and bottom edges. Let dry.

6. Trim any netting that hangs over the top or bottom edges of the shade with fabric scissors.

Make and Attach Ruffled Linen Strips

1. Decide how many vertical strips of linen to add to the shade. Work with an even number, as this makes spacing easy.

2. Iron the linen fabric. Using a rotary cutter, ruler, and cutting mat, cut strips of linen that are 1″ (2.5 cm) at the top, 2½″ (6.5 cm) at the bottom, and as long as the height of your shade, plus 2″ (5 cm) to accommodate the ruffling. For example, if your shade is 7″ (18 cm) high, cut the strips at least 9″ (23 cm) long.

3. With a sewing machine, baste along the length of each linen strip at the center, using a long stitch length. Do not backstitch at the beginning or end.

4. To ruffle a linen strip, grab a thread tail in one hand, and gently but firmly pull the linen away from that end. It will gather into a ruffle. Repeat at the other end of the strip.

5. With your fingers, distribute the gathers evenly along the length of the linen strip. Make sure the gathered strip fits the height of the shade exactly.

6. Knot the thread tails at the top and bottom of the linen strip and trim the excess thread.

7. Repeat steps 4 to 6 to ruffle all the linen strips. Apply fabric glue to the wrong side of the narrow end of a linen strip and adhere to the upper edge of the shade. Clip the strip in place with a clothespin.

8. Position the remaining ruffled linen strips evenly around the shade, placing the second ruffled strip directly across from the first one. Continue in this manner until all the ruffled strips have been glued to the shade. Let the glue dry.

9. When dry, use a stack of books or upturned bowl to raise the shade off the work surface.

10. Pull the ruffle strips flush to the lower rim of the shade. Apply fabric glue to the wrong side of the lower edge of each ruffle strip and press in place along the lower edge of the shade. Again, clip with clothespins. Repeat until all the strips have been glued in place. Let dry.

Finish Shade with Bias Tape or Ribbon

1. Cut two lengths of bias tape or ribbon: one to fit the top circumference of the shade, plus about 2″ (5 cm), and the other to fit the bottom circumference of the shade, plus about 2″ (5 cm).

2. Apply fabric glue along the upper front rim of the shade, across both the netting and linen. Also apply glue to the inside rim of the shade. Carefully position the bias tape or ribbon on the shade with half on the front of the shade and the rest folded over the upper edge to the inside of the shade. Trim the excess bias tape or ribbon 1″ (2.5 cm) past the starting point.

3. To finish the bias tape or ribbon, fold the end ½″ (1.5 cm) to the wrong side where it overlaps the beginning. Glue in place. Clip in place with clothespin until the glue is dry, and then remove the clothespin.

4. Repeat steps 2–3 along the lower edge of the shade, gluing several inches at a time. Use plenty of clothespins to keep the trim in place. Let dry, and then remove the clothespins.

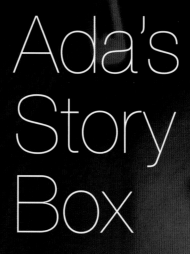

Ada's Story Box

When I was on the verge of becoming an aunt for the first time, I wanted to create a gift for my new niece that would help her to learn about her mother (my sister Robyn) from her family and some of her closest friends. So I decoupaged a wooden box with baby-themed images, then asked everyone to write "prompts" that would complete the sentence "Tell Ada a Story About ... " The result was a meaningful, personal "time capsule" of memories for Robyn and her daughter. This is a fun group project that can be adapted for all sorts of occasions in addition to births, such as engagements or weddings, graduations or the first day of school.

FINISHED DIMENSIONS

9" (23 cm) long x 6" (15 cm) wide x 1½"
(4 cm) high

MATERIALS

Cigar box
Decorative images from postcards,
 decorative paper, and/or color copies
 of copyright-free images
Vellum paper
Alphabet stamp set and other decorative
 stamps, if desired
Ink pad
Sheets of plain paper, cut to fit into the box
Pens
Paper scissors
Decoupage glue
Foam brush
Clear acrylic grid ruler

Make Story Box

1. Cut out decorative images from postcards, decorative paper, or color copies.

2. Play around with the placement of the images on the box before you glue them into place, leaving room on the front, as well as the inside lid, for a label. You can overlap images to create a collage. I like to leave some of the box showing.

3. When satisfied with the position of the elements, secure them to the box, one at a time, by applying a thin layer of decoupage glue to the back side, using a foam brush. Adhere each image to the box and smooth out any air bubbles or wrinkles with your hand. For overlapped images, adhere the under layers to the box first.

4. For the front label, cut several rectangles of vellum paper all the same size. My paper measured about 1″ (2.5 cm) high by 2½″ (6.5 cm) wide. Glue each layer in place with decoupage glue, staggering the layers to add some dimension. Make another label for the inside lid in the same manner. Let the labels dry.

5. Using the alphabet stamps, create a stamp that reads "A Story Box" and stamp the title onto the vellum label on the box front.

6. Using the alphabet stamps, create a stamp for the inside of the box that reads "Tell Ada (substitute the name of the baby) a Story About . . ." Stamp the wording onto the vellum label on the inside of the box front.

Create Story Prompts

1. Brainstorm ideas for "story prompts" about the parents or baby, so a parent can use the ideas as a starting point for a story. If desired, gather a group of family or friends to come up with the ideas. Story prompts may include trips the parents took, how they met, stories about grandparents or other family members, and so on.

2. Have everyone hand-write their prompts on paper cut to fit in the box. Decorate with stamps, if desired. Place the story prompts in box.

Pl. 85

A STORY BOX

Jewelry
Tree

Wood is one of my all-time favorite materials. I'm sure that it has something to do with growing up in a weathered old barn in Virginia. Here, a slice of wood embellished with a rub-on transfer corrals what would otherwise be an unruly jumble of jewelry. I like the contrast of the delicate rub-on transfer design against the wood's rough edges.

FINISHED DIMENSIONS

6" (15 cm) tall x 8" (20.5 cm) wide

MATERIALS

Wood slice with bark, foraged or purchased
   (available at craft stores)
Floral rub-on transfer (see Resources)
Decorative push-pin hooks or
   cabinet knobs
Screws to fit cabinet knobs and ¼" (6 mm)
   longer than depth of wood slice
   (if using cabinet knobs)
Sawtooth picture hanger with nails or
   nailess sawtooth hanger
Clear adhesive-backed rubber
   bumpers (optional)
Sandpaper (optional)
Scissors
Pencil
Bone folder or quarter
Drill with drill bit of appropriate size
   for cabinet knob screws
   (if using cabinet knobs)
Screwdriver (if using cabinet knobs)
Hammer

Add Design

1. If the wood slice has a rough surface, sand as necessary. Wipe off sanding dust.

2. Cut out rub-on transfer. Peel off backing and hold design over the wood slice until you like the placement. Set in place on the wood slice for layout purposes. Plan the placement of the push-pin hooks and mark their positions with a pencil.

3. Place the rub-on transfer, coated side down, in position on the wood slice. Transfer the design by rubbing over the top of the design with a bone folder or quarter. Be sure to rub completely over every part of the design.

4. Slowly peel up the transfer sheet, making sure that all parts of the design have transferred to the wood. If any part of the design remains on the plastic, lay the transfer sheet back down, aligning the design, and rub over the remaining image to transfer. Lift off the transfer sheet.

Add Hardware

1. If using decorative push-pin hooks, install them at the marked points. If using cabinet knobs, drill a hole at the marked points and install the cabinet knobs.

2. Attach a sawtooth picture hanger to the back of wood slice, using a hammer. If you placed the push pins or knobs off-center, you should hang the sawtooth off-center to the same side to balance the weight of your jewelry. If desired, adhere rubber bumpers to the back of the wood slice, placing one on each side, near the lower edge.

Foraging for Supplies

Walks and hikes are part of my weekend routine, probably because I live in a city where I can literally step out my door and pick up a trail without ever needing to get in a car. Within moments, I can trade sidewalks and traffic lights for tree canopies and silence. And when I'm lucky, I find supplies for projects along the way.

Try this and I'm sure you'll be surprised by the bounty you can pick up while hiking in the woods, down a dirt path, or even in the backyards of friends and family. Of course, you need to follow any guidelines that limit or forbid collecting and you need to ask permission when on private property. But, rest assured, there are plenty of places where you can collect acorns, pinecones, leaves, rocks, fallen branches, or wild berries that might inspire a project.

For instance, you might spot branches or tree stumps from which to slice wood for the Jewelry Tree (page 38). Or collect pinecones and other embellishments for the Willow Chandelier (page 88). Or gather leaves or flowers for the Pressed Flower Luminaria (page 80).

Even if you don't pick up anything tangible on your walks, if you're paying attention, you will certainly notice colors, shapes, and patterns that might work their way into a project. If you like, take along a small camera and sketchpad for note-taking.

Owen's Wall Art

After my nephew was born, I devoted one Saturday to making him a collage about adventure and exploration using decorative paper and attractive images I found in books. The key to this type of themed collage is to gather more material than you think you might need, and to give yourself the time to slowly build it so the sentiment and love shine through. Other occasions that could be celebrated with collage art include weddings, retirements, and birthdays.

24" x 30" (61 x 76 cm)

MATERIALS

Stretched canvas, 24" x 30" (61 x 76 cm) (or desired size)

Stash of decorative paper such as art paper, wrapping paper, and patterned tissue paper (one piece of paper should be large enough to cover the front and sides of the canvas); see notes below

Newspaper

Scissors

Decoupage glue

Bowl or plate to hold glue

Foam brush

Craft knife

Self-healing cutting mat

Pencil

NOTES: In addition to existing patterned papers, you can scan and print or make color photocopies of copyright-free artwork to include in your collage. Copyright-free images can be enlarged or reduced to fit the scale of your project.

I used mulberry paper for the background of my canvas. It has a lovely texture that takes on some translucency when you apply decoupage glue to it.

Create Background

1. Cover the work surface with newspaper to protect it from glue.

2. Cut a rectangle of paper for the background, cutting it 4" (10 cm) larger than the canvas in each direction so it can be folded over the sides.

3. Pour some decoupage glue into a bowl or onto a plate. With a foam brush, apply a thin but even layer of glue to the canvas front and then center the background rectangle of paper over the canvas. Use the heel of your hand to smooth out air bubbles and wrinkles, working from the center of the canvas out toward to the edges. If you're using a large canvas, you will likely have some wrinkles no matter how diligent you are smoothing out the paper. That's part of the charm of a large homemade collage.

4. Where the paper overhangs the edges of the canvas, snip each corner on a diagonal, from the outside corner of the paper to the edge of the canvas.

5. Working on one side at a time, prop the canvas upright on the work surface and apply a thin layer of glue to one side edge of the canvas. Fold the paper over the edge and press into place. When you reach a diagonally cut edge, apply glue to the adjacent side edge of the canvas, fold the excess corner paper around the edge, and glue in place. Continue in the same manner on the remaining sides. Let dry.

6. Using a craft knife or sharp scissors, trim any paper overhanging beyond the now-finished sides of the canvas.

Fill in Canvas

1. Cut out additional design elements, choosing elements that vary in size, color, and scale. Use some large blocks of color or pattern, and other stand-alone elements. Be sure to use a sharp craft knife so you are able to make precise cuts.

2. Arrange the elements on top of the canvas and play with the placement until you're satisfied with the design. When arranging a composition, I like to break up any solid lines or blocks of color with smaller elements to give the canvas visual interest.

3. When you're happy with the layout, lightly mark with a pencil the location of each piece. Be sure to make the mark in an area that will eventually be covered with paper. The elements will be glued on in order, from the bottom (closest to the canvas) to the top. You may want to mark in pencil on the back of each element the order in which you need to glue them on.

4. Glue the bottom-most elements in place first, letting them dry before gluing the next layer. Continue in this manner until all the elements are glued in place. Let dry completely. Trim any elements that overhang the canvas as necessary.

5. Apply several coats of decoupage glue over the entire canvas, letting the glue dry between coats.

Felt Adventure Mat

I made this reversible landscape mat after so many of my friends' kids became enchanted with the appliqués I had in my crafting stash. Blue with branches on one side and green with blades of grass on the other, it serves as a great backdrop for the imaginative scenes kids inevitably create. Storebought drawstring bags hold embroidered appliqués of birds, butterflies, and other natural elements; a decorated coffee can holds the mat and the bags when not in use.

MATERIALS

Two rectangles of felt: 1 sky blue and
    1 light green, at least 6½" x 15"
    (16.5 x 38 cm)
Scraps of brown felt
Scraps of grass-green felt
Thread to coordinate with felt colors
Empty coffee can
Decorative paper
Adhesive-backed paper for lid and
    front label
Iron-on embroidered appliqués, such
    as birds, leaves, flowers, and butterflies
One or more small muslin drawstring
    pouches or bags
Tracing paper or photocopy paper
Pencil
Chalk pencil or pen
Paper scissors
Fabric scissors
Straight pins
Sewing machine
Construction or scrap paper,
    for can template
Tape
Craft knife
Clear acrylic grid ruler
Self-healing cutting mat
Foam brush
Decoupage glue
Pen or marker to label can
Iron and ironing board

grass template
cut 1 of each

Make Felt Landscape

NOTE: Since you'll roll up the felt landscape and place it upright in the coffee can, you may need to adjust the height of the felt landscape depending on the size of the coffee can you're using. Make it as tall as the can, minus at least a half an inch to make sure it fits well.

1. From each of the sky-blue and light-green felt pieces, cut a rectangle measuring 6½" x 15" (16.5 x 38 cm) (or sized to fit your coffee can; see note above).

2. Trace or photocopy the branch and grass templates on page 51 and above onto paper and cut out.

3. Pin the branch template onto the brown felt and pin the grass templates onto the grass-green felt. Trace around the templates with a chalk pencil or pen. Cut inside the marked lines with fabric scissors.

4. Pin the felt grass pieces onto the light green felt rectangle, referring to the project photo opposite for placement. Allow the lower edges of the grass pieces to extend ½" (1.5 cm) beyond the edges of the felt rectangle. The excess will be trimmed off later. Pin the branches to the sky-blue felt rectangle, referring to the project photo on page 47 for placement. Allow the edge of the branch to extend ½" (1.5 cm) beyond the edge of the felt rectangle. The excess will be trimmed off later.

5. Sew the branch and grass pieces in place around the edges using a sewing machine, or hand-stitch in place.

6. Trim the excess from the branch and grass pieces so the edges are flush with the edges of the rectangles.

7. Pin the felt rectangles wrong sides together around the edges. Using a zigzag stitch, sew around the edges of the felt rectangles, backstitching at the beginning and end. Trim the thread tails.

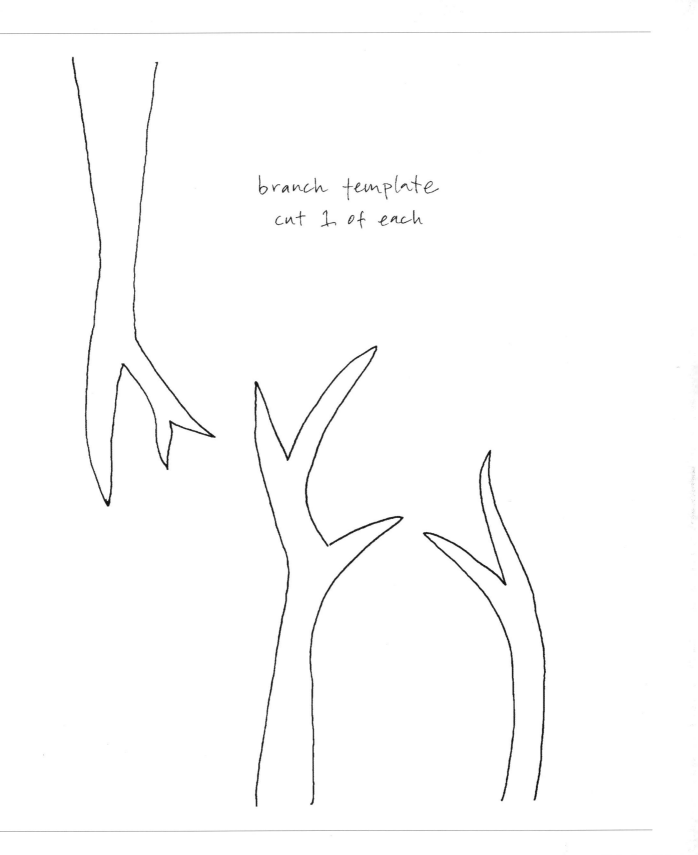

branch template
cut 1 of each

Make Template for Coffee Can Cover

1. Align one long edge of a piece of construction paper or scrap paper with the bottom edge of the coffee can and tape one short edge of the paper to the can. Wrap the paper around the can, marking where the paper overlaps the taped edge. Mark the paper along the upper edge of the can.

2. Untape the paper. Using a craft knife, grid ruler, and cutting mat, cut along the marked line. Make a cut where the edges overlap around can, cutting ½" (1.5 cm) beyond the mark for the overlap. Wrap the template around the can to check the fit and make any adjustments as necessary.

Cover Coffee Can

1. Lay the template on the decorative paper, making sure to take into account any pattern in the paper.

2. Trace the template onto the paper, using a ruler and pencil. Cut out, cutting just inside the marked line.

3. Using a foam brush, apply a thin layer of decoupage glue to the coffee can.

4. Place the paper on the can and wrap it around the can, so the ends overlap neatly. If the paper is skewed, quickly but carefully lift it off and try again.

5. When correctly aligned, press the paper flat against the can, using the heel of your hand to smooth out any air bubbles and ensure it lays flat.

6. Apply a thin layer of decoupage glue to the underside of the overlap and press in place.

7. When dry, apply a thin layer of decoupage glue to the front side of the paper as a sealant.

Decorate Lid

1. Place the lid upside down on adhesive-backed paper and trace with a pencil.

2. Cut just inside the marked line. If the lid has a ridge along the outer edge, trim off an amount equal to the width of the ridge, so the paper will fit in the space inside the ridge.

3. Peel the backing off the circle and press onto the center of the lid.

4. Write a message or title on the label to identify the contents of the can, or add a personal note.

Finish and Assemble

1. Using an iron, fuse an embroidered appliqué to the front of the muslin bag(s), following the manufacturer's instructions.

2. Place the remaining embroidered appliqués in the muslin bag(s). Roll up the felt landscape panel and place the felt roll and muslin bag inside the covered coffee can.

Homemade Popsicles

I vividly remember making homemade Popsicles as a kid. My sisters, cousins, and I would pour storebought lemonade into little paper cups, add a Popsicle stick when the lemonade started to get slushy, and muster up the patience we needed to wait for everything to freeze thoroughly.

I don't think there's anything wrong with that method, through these days my recipe is a little more creative. I puree ripe fruit into liquid form, add sugar if needed, pour the mixture into Popsicle molds or paper cups, freeze until slushy (usually a couple of hours), then insert wooden sticks and freeze until solid. If I'm making Popsicles for grownups, sometimes I add a splash of liquor.

At left are a few of the flavor combinations I've come to love. I tend to follow the seasons and make Popsicles from whatever fruit is ripe.

MY FAVORITE FLAVORS

Summer peaches, pureed with blueberries and a splash of orange juice (or rum)

Fresh berries, green tea, and honey

Local strawberries with a dash of cinnamon (or skip the cinnamon and add tequila or rum)

Ripe cantaloupe with whole raspberries

Gilded End
Table

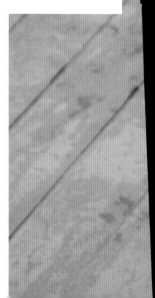

I fell for the minimal lines of this side table as soon as I spotted it one Saturday morning in a junky antique shop near my home. Its wooden top was sun-bleached and stained, but it wasn't warped, so I covered it with hand-blocked "gilded" paper and sealed it with several coats of special Mod Podge to protect it from damage. This technique will work on any flat surface, such as the insides of trays or the tops of larger tables.

FINISHED DIMENSIONS

15" (38 cm) long x 15" (38 cm) wide x 17"
(43 cm) high

MATERIALS

Table with flat top
Decorative paper to fit table
Wood stain
Decoupage glue (see note below)
Paper towels or rags
400-grit sandpaper
Painter's tape
2 foam brushes
Pencil
Craft knife
Clear acrylic grid ruler
Self-healing cutting mat

NOTE: I use ordinary decoupage glue to
apply the decorative paper to the tabletop.
To protect the paper after it is applied
(step 8), I like to use Hard Coat Mod Podge
by Plaid because it forms an especially
hard, water-resistant surface.

Prepare Table

1. Wipe the table with a damp paper towel or rag to remove any dust or dirt. Sand the table surface, if necessary, and wipe away sanding dust. Let dry completely.

2. Using painter's tape, tape around the underside of the table-top at the edge to catch any drips from the stain.

3. Apply stain to the edges of the table with a foam brush. Add extra coats of stain to the sides if desired to darken the color. Wipe off excess stain with a paper towel or rag and let dry completely.

Apply Paper and Seal

1. Position decorative paper wrong side up on a work surface. Place the table upside down on the decorative paper and trace around the edges of the tabletop with a pencil.

2. Remove the table and cut just inside the marked lines using a craft knife, ruler, and cutting mat.

3. Lay the paper on the tabletop and check the fit. The edges of the paper should be flush with the edges of the table and not extend over the sides of the table. If the paper is too big, mark and trim accordingly.

4. Using painter's tape, tape off the side edges of the table, just below the top edge.

5. Starting in one corner of the table, apply decoupage glue with a clean foam brush. Align a corner of the paper with a corner of the table.

6. Continue applying glue to the table and paper to glue a few inches at a time, pressing out any bubbles or air pockets in the paper as you work. Repeat until the paper covers the tabletop.

7. Apply glue to the edges and corners of the paper and press securely into place. Let dry.

8. Apply a layer of decoupage glue (this is where I use Hard Coat Mod Podge) to the tabletop. Let dry. Dampen 400-grit sandpaper with water, lightly sand the top of the table and wipe dry. To build up a durable top coat, apply a total of four to five layers of Hard Coat Mod Podge, sanding between applications.

Glam Leather Cuff

The simple tapered shape of this cuff makes for an intriguing stacked effect when wrapped around the wrist. It's a statement piece, but a comfortable one. I gave it a glamorous edge by using leather with a metallic finish and an ornate button.

About 2" (5 cm) wide x 15½"
(39.5 cm) long

MATERIALS

Strip of leather, at least 5" x 18"
    (12.5 x 45.5 cm)
Decorative shank button, ½" (1.5 cm)
    in diameter
Thread to match leather
Tracing paper
Paper scissors
Pen
Sharp fabric scissors
Chalk pencil
Self-healing cutting mat
Craft knife
Clear acrylic grid ruler

Cut Leather

1. Photocopy the leather cuff templates opposite, cut out, and tape together where indicated, butting the ends (not overlapping them).

2. Place the cuff template on the right side of the leather and trace around the edge of the template with a pen.

3. Using fabric scissors, cut just inside the marked line.

Add Closure

1. Thread a needle with thread and knot the ends together. Sew the button to the marked point, beginning by bringing the needle up from the wrong side, so knot is on wrong side of leather.

2. I've indicated buttonhole placement on template, but make sure this works for you before cutting. To do so, rub chalk onto the top of the button. Wrap the cuff around your wrist, pressing the narrow end of the cuff on top of the button. This will transfer a chalk mark to the wrong side of the cuff to serve as a guide for the buttonhole.

3. Unwrap the cuff and lay it flat on the cutting mat.

4. Create a buttonhole by making a slit $\frac{1}{8}$" (3 mm) longer than the button diameter, centered over the chalk mark, using a craft knife and ruler. Test-fit the button into the slit and adjust the length of the slit as necessary.

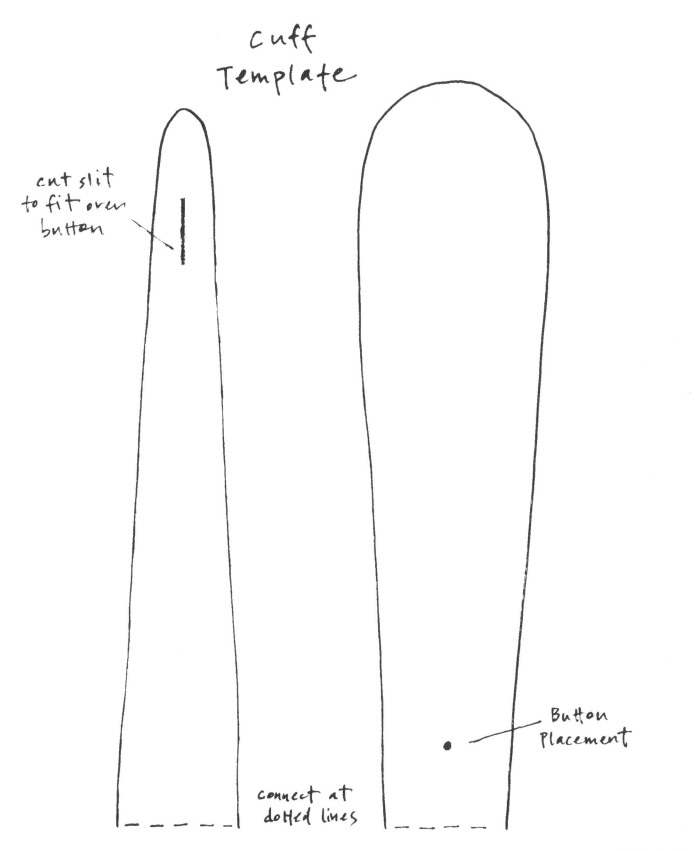

Cuff
Template

cut slit
to fit over
button

connect at
dotted lines

Button
Placement

grow

chapter 2

aking these salves is an easy process that involves infusing oil with your chosen herb or herbs, then combining the oil with beeswax. Although oils can be infused in a couple hours on the stove, I prefer to infuse them using the slower solar method, which takes a couple of weeks. Watching the sun glint through the jars of golden oil as they steep is beautiful—and makes the wait worthwhile.

My ideal is to make these salves with herbs I've grown in my garden and then dried myself, but high-quality dried herbs purchased from a bulk supplier (see Resources on page 146) work well also. Use these emollient salves on hands, feet, elbows, or any other part of your body that needs moisturizing.

Herbal Salves

YIELD

About 2 cups (473 mL)

MATERIALS

Dried herbs or fragrant flowers

About 2 cups (473 mL) olive oil or other
carrier oil, such as calendula oil or
almond oil

About 1 cup (236.5 mL) beeswax
(you can use a small votive beeswax
candle if you can't find pure beeswax)

Essential oil (optional)

Clean glass jars with tight-fitting lids,
for infusing oil

Cheesecloth or a jelly bag

Liquid ingredient measuring cup

Saucepan

Grater

Plate

Tablespoon

Spoon

Saucer

Small clean tins or jars with lids

Kraft paper adhesive labels and printed
Japanese *washi* tape (see Resources),
for labels (optional)

Infuse Oil

NOTE: When you're infusing the oils, there is no strict measurement or ratio of herbs to oil—just make sure to use enough oil to generously cover the herbs, since the herbs will absorb some of the oil.

1. Place the dried herbs or flowers in a clean jar and cover with olive or other carrier oil, filling to within 1″ (2.5 cm) of the top of the jar.

2. Seal the jar tightly and place in a sunny window. Shake every day or so for two weeks to disperse the herbs throughout the oil.

3. Place a double layer of cheesecloth or a jelly bag over the measuring cup. Pour the contents of the jar over the cheesecloth or jelly bag to strain out the herbs. Let drain.

4. When the oil stops dripping, wring the herbs out with your hands to extract all of the infused oil. Discard spent herbs. Note how much infused oil you have in the measuring cup.

Create Salve

1. Pour the infused oil into a small saucepan. Grate the beeswax onto a plate. For every ¼ cup (59 mL) of infused oil in the pan, add 2 tablespoons of grated beeswax to the pan and stir until dissolved. If you're using essential oil, add a couple drops for every 2 tablespoons (29.5 mL) of infused oil, or more if you prefer a stronger scent.

2. Warm the ingredients gently over low heat. Meanwhile, place a saucer in the freezer.

3. When the wax is dissolved, remove the pan from the heat and place a spoonful of the salve mixture onto the cold saucer. Place the saucer back in the freezer.

4. After about a minute, check the consistency of the salve by removing the saucer from the freezer and testing it with your finger. If it's very hard, add more infused oil. If it's too soft, add more grated beeswax. Aim for a consistency that will work well as a salve (I prefer mine on the creamy side so I can use it as a heavy-duty gardening balm).

5. When the salve reaches the desired consistency, pour it into clean tins or jars.

6. Place the tins or jars on a level surface to cool and set. When the salve has cooled completely, place lids on the tins or jars.

Add Labels

1. Add decorative labels to the tins or jars to identify the blends. I printed the blend names on adhesive kraft labels and cut the labels to fit the tops of the tins. I also added a piece of *washi* tape along one side. For more label ideas, see page 71.

2. Store the salve in a cool, dark place.

Beekeeping

My sister Brooke lived and worked on an apple orchard for several years, and one spring I visited while a local beekeeper hauled his hives out among the apple blossoms to pollinate all the trees. That was the first time I really comprehended that most of the fruit and veggies we eat are pollinated by bees. It's almost like science fiction: armies of tiny insects traveling from bloom to bloom, gathering and spreading the pollen that coaxes blossoms into tasty fruit and vegetables.

A couple of years later, when I learned that there was a local beekeeping group in San Francisco, I pounced. I went to meetings and found out I could tend my hives on weekends, so I bought the getup and ordered the bees. When I went to pick them up one Sunday, the club president handed me a screened box with about eight thousand humming bees clumped around the queen and—the part I wasn't prepared for—a couple dozen bees clinging to the outside of the box. She told me not to worry, and I didn't want to look like a wimp newbie, so I took the box with my bare hands and headed for my car. That's when a longtime beekeeper called after me, "Hey, you're a beekeeper now!" and I straightened up a little, feeling silently proud and thrilled. But I'll never forget driving home with the windows down, checking the rearview mirror every other second.

My first year of beekeeping was a pretty wild ride. Like most things in life, alongside the wide-eyed wonder, there was also heartbreak. I had a failed queen, disease, and the stomach-punch to all beekeepers: swarming. That's when, despite all your best efforts, half the bees up and leave. As a result, my harvest was pretty skimpy. But still, the first weekend I pulled frames out of the hive that were heavy with honey and warmed by the sun, I felt victorious. Beekeeping is nothing if not truly awe-inspiring.

So if you want to give beekeeping a try or just want to pick up some local beeswax or honey, ask around. With the skyrocketing popularity of beekeeping in rural and urban neighborhoods alike, odds are pretty decent that you might live near a beekeeper. And most beekeepers I know are only too happy to share the gospel and byproducts of their hobby. See Resources on page 146 for more information.

Fresh Botanic Spritzers

Generally I'm pretty barebones when it comes to a beauty regimen, but I'm definitely a sucker for botanic spritzers. I spray myself with a chilled cucumber spritzer when it's hot and I want to be refreshed. Lavender is great for winding down, and cucumber helps me perk up.

YIELD

About 1 quart (1 liter)

MATERIALS

For spritzer:
Fresh cucumber, citrus fruit, fragrant
    flowers, lavender, and/or other herbs
Distilled water (see note below)
Glass spray bottles or atomizers
Knife
Dry ingredient measuring cup
Pitcher or large liquid ingredient
    measuring cup
Fine-mesh sieve
Bowl
Funnel

For labels:
Ink pads in two colors
Decorative botanical stamp
Rubber alphabet stamp kit
Scrap paper
Round, white adhesive labels

NOTE: Spritzers are traditionally made
with distilled water as a base. For variety,
you might also want to try green tea or aloe
vera juice.

Make Spritzer

NOTE: You may want to experiment to figure out your preferred ratio of botanicals to liquid. This will determine the strength of the scent. I usually use about 1–2 cups (236.5–473 mL) of fresh botanicals per quart (liter) of liquid.

1. Choose fresh botanicals for your spritzer as desired. Slice any fruits or vegetables into thin slices and roughly tear any herbs. Place the botanicals in a pitcher or large liquid ingredient measuring cup.

2. Pour water over your botanical mixture and let steep in the refrigerator for several hours.

3. Strain the botanical mixture over a bowl, being careful to strain out all the organic materials to avoid spoilage. Reserve the scented liquid.

4. Pour the scented liquid into a spray bottle, using a funnel. Store the spritzer in the refrigerator for up to a couple weeks— the spray is especially revitalizing when it's cold.

Make Labels

1. Load ink onto the botanical stamp and stamp the image onto adhesive labels. Let dry.

2. Arrange the alphabet stamps to spell out the name of the mixture. Alphabet stamps sometimes require you to set the letters backward and upside down, so test a few letters on scrap paper first to make sure you get the hang of the alignment.

3. Load contrasting ink onto the alphabet stamp. Center the stamp over the label and stamp the lettering.

4. Peel the backing off the label and apply the label to the glass spray bottle.

Easy Handmade Labels

I am a sucker for beautiful packaging, whether it's for pots of jam or honey or boxes or tubes of beauty lotions and potions. And while I can't often replicate the packaging I admire in stores, when I'm working on my own projects at home, especially ones that I plan to give away, I try to make time to finish them with at least a pretty label.

I usually pick up my label-making supplies at standard office-supply, art, and craft stores. I always keep sheets of 8½" x 11" (21.5 x 28 cm) adhesive labels on hand because they can be cut to any shape and size. This comes in especially handy for jam jar lids, since I've never found plain, precut labels in the right size. Just take the top screw part of the top, turn upside down on a piece of adhesive label and trace inside the inner circles with a pencil. Cut, decorate, and apply to the lid. While office supply stores may only stock white labels, art and craft stores often sell them in a wide range of colors, including my favorite, kraft paper brown—that lovely color of plain grocery bags that looks beautiful on any project.

Paper luggage tags with strings are another staple of mine. So is Japanese *washi* tape, which is similar to masking tape but comes in bright colors and patterns. I like to run a strip of the tape along the short edge of a label to add some pattern and color.

To decorate labels, I often rely on rubber stamps, especially my alphabet stamps. A workhorse in my collection is a self-inking rubber stamp with changeable type. I have to use a pair of tweezers to hand-set this type—which takes a little bit of time—but I love the result. Or I skip the stamps and hand-write on my label with a Sharpie pen. Done neatly, a handwritten label can sometimes feel even more personal and thoughtful than anything else.

Herbed Bath Salts & Shower Scrub

Weekend afternoons, I try to make time for a long soak in the tub with a book or the weekend papers. Adding scented bath salts makes it more indulgent. And a home-made salt scrub invigorates the daily shower routine. The scrub is rich with moisturizing almond oil.

YIELD

Shower scrub: 1 cup (236.5 mL)
Bath salts: 5 cups (1183 mL)

MATERIALS

For both shower scrub and bath salts:
Non-plastic mixing bowl
Large spoon or scoop
Glass jars or containers with tight-fitting lids
    (plastic will absorb oils)
Essential oils and/or finely ground dried
    flowers or herbs
Tablespoon (measuring spoon)

For shower scrub:
½ cup (146 g) Epsom salts
¼ cup (30.5 g) almond oil
¼ cup (30.5 g) cornmeal

For bath salts:
3 cups (876 g) Epsom salts
2 cups (461 g) coarse sea salt

For labels:
Round, white adhesive labels to fit the
    lid on the container
Pressed flowers (press your own
    or purchase them from craft store;
    to press your own see Pressed
    Flower Luminaria project on page
    80 for instructions)
Paintbrush
Decoupage glue

Make Shower Scrub

1. Combine salts, oil, and cornmeal in non-plastic bowl until well mixed.

2. Add essential oil and/or ground flowers or herbs until you're satisfied with the strength of the fragrance and the distribution of the added materials (I use several drops of essential oils and 1–2 tablespoons (15–29.5 mL) of dried flowers for each batch).

3. Scoop the mixture into glass jars and close the lids.

Make Bath Salts

NOTE: I add dried herbs and flowers to bath salts, which means there will be floating bits of dried flowers in the bath. If you're not crazy about that idea, skip the dried flowers or herbs and stick to the essential oils.

1. Mix salts in non-plastic bowl until well-mixed.

2. Add several drops of essential oil and/or ground flowers or herbs until you're satisfied with the strength of the fragrance and the distribution of the added materials.

3. Scoop the salt mixture into glass jars and close the lids.

Make Labels

1. Remove the round label from the backing and place on top of the jar lid.

2. With a paintbrush, apply a thin layer of decoupage glue on top of the label.

3. Position a dried flower on the label and let dry.

4. Apply a thin layer of decoupage glue on top of the flower. You may need to gently apply glue under any loose petals, to ensure they lay flat. Let dry.

5. Apply a second layer of decoupage glue to the flower to seal it in place. Let dry.

Winter Marmalade

I make my Winter Marmalade with Seville oranges for a bright, bittersweet flavor, but you can use any winter citrus: grapefruit, blood oranges, or lemons.

If you've never canned before, don't be scared to give it a whirl–like me, you might become addicted. There are few things more satisfying than hearing the victorious pops that mean your jars have sealed. Well, there's also the pleasure of gazing upon the jewel-colored jars on the shelf, of giving them away to friends and family, and, of course, eating the contents.

YIELD

Six or seven 12-ounce (355 mL) jars

MATERIALS

2½ pounds (1.15 kg) Seville oranges
4 pints (1.9 L) water
4 pounds (1.8 kg) sugar
⅓ cup (79 mL) lemon juice
Knife
Citrus juicer or reamer
Large bowl
Liquid ingredient measuring cup
Large, heavy-bottomed saucepan,
    at least 4-quart (3.8 L) capacity
Large pot for sterilizing and processing
    jars, with a rack or folded towel set
    in the bottom
Large metal spoon
Six or seven 12-ounce (355 mL) glass
    preserving jars with 2-piece lids
Small saucer
Potholder or oven mitt
Jar lifter or tongs
Papertowels

NOTE: For more information about safe canning read the USDA Canning Guidelines online—www.foodsaving.com.

Prepare Fruit

1. Cut the oranges in half and squeeze the juice into a large bowl. Pick out and discard the seeds.

2. Trim the rinds into thick or thin strips, depending on your preference (and patience).

3. Add the rinds, including the membranes and any pulp, to the large bowl with the juice and cover with 4 pints (1.9 L) water. Leave covered for 24 hours (this step ensures the peel will soften properly when cooking the marmalade).

Cook Marmalade and Prepare Jars

1. The next day, pour the entire contents of the bowl into a large saucepan (be sure the pan has plenty of extra room—you will need it when the marmalade is boiling and sputtering.

2. Bring the contents of the pan to a boil, and then gently simmer, covered, stirring occasionally, until the peel is soft and the liquid is reduced by one-quarter to one-third, at least two hours. Check to make sure the peel is tender by scooping a rind from the pan, allowing it to cool slightly, and squishing it in your fingers. If it doesn't squish easily, it isn't ready.

3. When the marmalade is almost ready (the peel is tender), cover the jars with water in a large pot.

4. Place a small saucer in the freezer. You'll use this to test whether the marmalade will set properly.

5. When the peel is soft, add the sugar and lemon juice and stir to dissolve.

6. Turn up the heat and bring the mixture to a boil, stirring occasionally, but be sure the sugar is totally dissolved before cranking up the heat, or any un-dissolved sugar will burn at the bottom of the pan.

7. When the marmalade reaches a rapid boil, let it boil for 20–25 minutes without stirring, and then start testing to see if it has set. To test the marmalade, move the pan off the heat, place a small spoonful of the marmalade onto the cold saucer, and place the saucer in the freezer. After a minute, remove the saucer and push the marmalade with your finger: If the surface crinkles, the marmalade has reached its setting point. If there are no wrinkles, return the pan to the heat and continue to rapidly boil, checking it every 5 minutes to see if it has set.

8. Meanwhile, while the marmalade is boiling, turn on the heat under the jars in water, bring to a boil, and boil for at least 10 minutes.

9. When the marmalade reaches its setting point, remove the pot from the heat and let stand for no more than 5 minutes. This lets the marmalade thicken so the rind will be evenly distributed in jars. Cover the flat lids with simmering water. Remove the jars to a folded towel on the counter using a jar lifter or tongs (no need to dry off). Don't remove lids from simmering water yet.

Fill and Seal Jars

1. Working quickly but carefully, ladle marmalade into the hot jars. Fill to 1/4" (6 mm) beneath the top rim. Wipe any marmalade from the threads and rims of the jars with a paper towel.

2. Drain the flat lids and place them on top of the jars, white sides down, and tighten the rings by hand to seal.

3. Using tongs or jar lifter, return the jars, upright, to a rack or folded towel set inside the pot you boiled the jars in. Make sure they're covered with water by at least 1" (2.5 cm) and bring the water to a boil. Boil for 5 minutes, then return the jars to the towel on the counter and let cool completely.

4. As the marmalade cools, the jars will vacuum-seal. You will know the jars are properly sealed when you press on the lid and it does not depress any further. If it does depress and clicks down with the force of your finger, it has not sealed properly. Refrigerate any jars that don't vacuum-seal and use within two weeks.

Summer Bachelor's Jam

Bachelor's Jam, which I first learned about in Pam Corbin's wonderful book *Preserves*, isn't really jam at all. It's a way to preserve summer fruit by covering it with rum or any other spirit, and letting it infuse until the December holidays, when you can add the fruity alcohol to festive drinks, and the soaked fruit to desserts. I like to think of it as a slow, tipsy maceration.

Start in the summer by placing ripe, clean fruit, such as berries and sliced stone fruit (e.g., peaches and plums), in the bottom of an earthenware bowl (do not use plastic or metal). For every 1 cup (about 150 g or 236.5 mL) of fruit, add ½ cup (100 g) of sugar and let it macerate for about an hour. Then add enough rum to cover the fruit. Place a plate on top of the fruit to keep it submerged, then cover the bowl with plastic wrap and leave at room temperature. As fruit comes into season, add to the bowl along with enough rum to keep it covered. Keep this going throughout the summer, and when you're done, let the whole shebang sit until the holidays. When you're ready to serve, stir everything together, then strain off the liquid. Try it mixed with fizzy water or ginger ale, add a dash to Champagne, or serve it straight. Spoon the boozy fruit over ice cream.

Pressed Flower Luminaria

These lanterns give off a soft, ethereal light, perfect for adding glow to outdoor gatherings or indoor suppers. They also show off dried flowers in a spare, modern way–pressed between gauzy panels made from wax paper. As twilight fades to night, the luminaria glow brighter and brighter.

FINISHED DIMENSIONS

4½" (11.5 cm) cube

MATERIALS

Foraged flowers or foliage, such as ferns, leaves, rock rose, and Queen Anne's Lace (see note below)
Wax paper
Japanese washi tape (paper tape)
Votive candle in glass holder or battery-operated flameless LED tealight candle
Paper towels
Heavy books or a flower press
Craft knife
Clear acrylic grid ruler
Self-healing cutting mat
Iron and ironing board

NOTE: Delicate leaves and flowers will dry faster than other types of specimens. Choose specimens that will allow a lot of contact between the sheets of wax paper so the sheets will adhere to each other.

Press Floral Materials

Arrange freshly picked floral materials flat between two paper towels, and then place the paper towels between the pages of a heavy book or flower press. If using a book, stack other books on top to weigh down. Let dry completely. This will take a few days.

Make Panels

1. Using a craft knife, cut four 9 x 4 ½" (23 x 11.5 cm) rectangles of wax paper.

2. Set iron to medium. When hot, place a flower or foilage on one side of the wax paper rectangle. You will fold the other half on top and seal to create a square panel, so arrange the flower or foliage within the rectangle accordingly. Keep in mind you can place the flower or foliage so it runs beyond the edge of the paper since you can trim after making the sealed wax paper square.

3. Fold the rectangle of wax paper in half to create a square so the pressed item is sandwiched between the two layers of wax paper. Press along the folded edge with your finger, making sure the edges are aligned.

4. Seal with the iron, pressing over the wax paper lightly and quickly. The iron will fuse the two pieces of wax paper into one sheet.

5. Repeat steps 2–4 so you have four sealed square panels. Trim, if necessary.

Create Lanterns

1. Lay two floral panels side-by-side with right sides up and edges touching. Orient the panels as you want them to appear in the finished lantern.

2. Cut a 5" (12.5 cm) length of Japanese washi tape. Center the tape over the join between the panels and press in place, letting the tape extend ¼" (6 mm) at the ends. Flip the floral panels over and press the tape ends to the wrong sides of the panels.

3. Fold the panels, wrong sides together, at the join and run your fingers along the fold to make a sharp crease in the tape. This will allow the panels to be positioned at 90-degree angles in the finished lantern.

4. Continue joining the remaining floral panels in the same manner to make a floral sleeve. For the final join you may need to adjust how you tape the panels together by placing the tape along one edge of a panel so half of its width overhangs, and then attaching the neighboring panel.

5. Set the floral sleeve in the desired location and then place a votive candle in a glass holder or LED tealight in the center of the sleeve.

have always envied people who can draw realistically and beautifully–alas, I am not one of them. But my lack of drawing skills has inspired me to find other ways to portray images on paper, such as stamping, transferring, and, as shown here, rubbing. For this project, I like to keep the overall effect delicate, with a light hand and a graceful sweep of dotted swirly lines in the background.

FINISHED SIZE

4" (10 cm) long x 5½" (14 cm) wide

MATERIALS

Pressed flowers or foliage (see note below)
Tracing or vellum paper (a tablet works well)
Colored pencils
Pencil sharpener
4" x 5½" (10 x 14 cm) blank note cards
    and envelopes (or size desired)
Self-healing cutting mat
Ruler
Pencil
Craft knife
Ballpoint pen
Eraser
Glue stick
Heavy stack of books

NOTE: Sturdy ferns and leaves, such as ginkgo, work well for this project. Look for specimens with strong veins and relief that will transfer with the colored pencils.

Botanical
Note Cards

Press Floral Materials

Arrange freshly picked floral materials flat between two paper towels, then place the paper towels between the pages of a heavy book or flower press. If using a book, stack other books on top to weigh down. Let dry completely. This will take a few days.

Make Botanical Rubbings

1. Do a test rubbing by placing a flower or leaf on a work surface so the side with the most visible veins or detail faces up (usually the underside of a leaf). Place a clean sheet of tracing paper or vellum on top. Use the side of a colored pencil to color over the plant material. Make a couple samples and experiment with the amount of pressure you apply to the pencil. Try a light wash of color and a heavy application of color to see what you like best.

2. After making a test rubbing, select a pressed flower or leaf for your project and place the specimen so the side with the most visible veins or detail faces up. Place a clean sheet of tracing paper on top. I make my rubbings within my tablet of tracing paper—the paper stays in place since it's still bound at the top, and the papers below provide a good, flat working surface.

3. If you're using two colored pencils, one for the outline of the plant material and another for the interior, sharpen the pencil for the outline. Using the outline color, trace around the outer edges of the plant material.

4. Choose a dull-tipped pencil for the interior and apply color to the interior of the outline, using the side of the pencil to give an even wash of color.

5. Lift the paper. If you've missed any spots, go back and gently fill them in.

Trim to Size

1. Working on a self-healing cutting mat, place the paper with the rubbing over a blank card. Move the rubbing until you're satisfied with the layout (I like my rubbings to be bleed off one edge of the card).

2. When you like the position, place a ruler on top of the paper with the rubbing, along the edge of the note card, and transfer a line corresponding to the edge of the note card onto the paper with the rubbing. Repeat with other three sides to transfer the outline of the entire card onto the tracing paper or vellum.

3. Remove the card from underneath the rubbing and cut the tracing paper or vellum, just inside the marked lines.

Add Dot Detail

1. To add the dot detail, draw loops, lines, or even the outline of a simple flower onto the front of the card with a pencil.

2. Using a ballpoint pen, make a series of dots along the pencil markings. Let dry, then erase the pencil lines.

Assemble Card

1. To assemble the card, apply a thin, even layer of glue stick to the front of the card, being sure to glue up to the edges of the card.

2. Place the paper with the rubbing on top of the card and press in place with your fingers.

3. Place the card under a heavy stack of books and let dry completely.

Willow Chandelier

While pinecones and antique holiday ornaments float down from this hanging decoration, there's nothing traditionally seasonal about it. Take it outdoors for warm weekend suppers with friends, or hang it above an indoor table when the weather turns cooler for an enchanted forest feeling.

FINISHED DIMENSIONS

Wreath: 15" (38 cm) wide x 26" (66 cm)
long x 3" (7.5 cm) deep
Hanging elements: 4–8" (10–20.5 cm) long

MATERIALS

Bendable branches, such as willow
    (see note below), about 16–20 clip-
    pings, each 1–3' (30.5–91.5 cm) long
Brown wrapped floral wire (I used 26-gauge)
Embellishments, such as pinecones and
    holiday ornaments, to hang from
    the chandelier
Jewelry crimp tubes, approximately 2 mm
    (available in beading section of most
    craft stores)
4 yards of grosgrain ribbon, ³⁄₈" (1 cm)
    wide or whatever width you desire
Pruning shears
Wire cutters
Scissors
Monofilament fishing line
Needle-nose pliers
Small screw eyes (optional, if using pine
    cones or objects without a hole to
    thread monofilament line through)
Screw hook for hanging
Toggle bolt (for plaster or wallboard ceilings)
Drill and drill bit for ceiling hook (if required)

NOTE: If you want to do some pruning on
your trees, look for branches that are
young and flexible. Alternatively, parks
department folks and neighbors are usually
happy for you to take some branches off
their hands after they've pruned. Or find a
well-stocked florist or flower market and
buy branches. I used willow branches.
When the branches dry in a couple weeks,
they usually darken. The thinner the
branches, the more flexible they are, so if
you find it difficult to work with your
branches, cut the thick ends off using
pruning shears.

Make Oval Wreath

1. Divide branches into two equal bundles.

2. Cut several 36″ (91.5 cm) pieces of floral wire.

3. Working with one bundle of branches at a time, wrap the branches together with floral wire at several locations to secure. A quick and easy way to do this is to fold the wire in half, wrap the folded wire around the bundle of branches twice, and pass the cut ends through the folded end of the wire. Pull the cut ends tight against the loop to tighten the wire around the branches. Then pull the cut ends around the branches in the opposite direction, and twist the ends around a branch to secure. Cut the excess wire close to the branches. Repeat with the other bundle of branches.

4. Cut several more pieces of floral wire.

5. Working with someone else who can provide another pair of hands, place the thin end of one bundle of branches against the thick end of the other bundle. Secure the bundles together in the same manner as before to make one long bundle of branches.

6. Bend the bundle of branches at several points to turn the bundle into an oval or circular shape, and secure with floral wire as before.

String Hanging Elements

1. Cut as many lengths of monofilament line as you have items to hang. I cut the the line between 12″ (30.5 cm) and 15″ (38 cm) long.

2. For items such as ornaments or oversize buttons, string one end of the line through the hanger or hole. Place a crimp on the long tail of the line and slide it down toward the hole in the item you're hanging. Insert the short end of the line into the crimp, so the crimp contains both ends of the line. With pliers, flatten the crimp. Trim the short tail just above where it emerges from the crimp.

3. Thread the long end of the line up through the branches, wrapping it around a branch at the top of the oval. Secure in place with a double knot. Trim the excess.

4. Continue to hang additional elements from the oval in the same manner as first one, spacing the elements evenly around the oval and varying the lengths of the line. For items that do not have a hole, such as pinecones, install a small screw eye into top of item and secure line to the screw eye.

Hang Chandelier

1. Cut four lengths of grosgrain ribbon, each about 3′ (91.5 cm)long.

2. Tie a length of ribbon to the center of each side of the wreath, spacing the ribbons around the circle or oval evenly. Secure with a double knot and trim the excess off the short tail. Repeat with the other three ribbons.

3. Pull the long ribbon ends upward, above the decoration, to meet in the center of the oval. Lift the chandelier to make sure it hangs level. If not, move the ribbon placement until it hangs correctly.

4. Gather all the ends and tie into a double knot. Trim the excess ribbon.

5. If hanging inside, screw a hook into the ceiling, using a toggle bolt, if required, and following the manufacturer's instructions. Place the knot over the hook to hang the chandelier. If hanging outside, thread a length of monofilament line through the central, top knot of ribbons. Wrap the other end around a tree bough and hang.

Wine Bottle Terrarium

Green up any desktop or bare corner with this simple terrarium—or a pair. To transform your own bottle into a terrarium, all you need is a simple bottle cutting kit, generally available at craft stores. Or, if you prefer, you can make your terrariums out of store-bought glass containers, such as vases or hurricanes. Look for thick cork stoppers to fit the wine bottle terrarium at brewing supply stores.

FINISHED SIZES

Wine bottle container: 5" (12.5 cm) high x 3" (7.5 cm) diameter
Tall glass: 7" (18 cm) high x 5" (12.5 cm) diameter

MATERIALS

Empty glass bottle, such as a wine bottle or other glass container, such as a vase
Glass bottle cutting kit, if using a bottle (comes with candle, sandpaper, and polishing powder)
Pea gravel or pebbles
Activated charcoal (find this where aquariums are sold)
Sphagnum moss
Pre-mixed terrarium soil or good-quality potting soil with builders sand and humus (two parts potting soil to one part each of sand and humus)
Small, slow-growing plants such as air plants, miniature ferns, succulants, or moss (ask your local nursery for suggestions)
Tapered cork stopper (if you plan to use plants, such as moss, that require a humid environment)
Dish soap
Newspapers
Protective eyewear (if cutting a bottle)
Spray mister filled with water

Cut Bottle

NOTE: If not using a wine bottle, skip to "Build Terrarium."

1. Wash the glass bottle with dish soap and let dry. Cover your work surface with newspapers to catch any thin shards of glass that may be produced while cutting. Put on protective eyewear.

2. Cut the glass bottle about 5″ (12.5 cm) above the base, following the manufacturer's instructions. Most hobby kits use a tool to score the glass, followed by heating and cooling to crack the glass. You may find that you need to repeat the heating and cooling steps a few more times than the directions suggest, but don't let this discourage you from trying it—cutting glass is a quick and easy process. Following the manufacturer's instructions, polish the cut edge of the glass with polishing powder.

3. When finished with the cutting and polishing, carefully discard the newspapers with glass shards.

Build Terrarium

1. Cover the work surface with a layer of newspaper and set the glass container in the center. Add ½″ (1.5 cm) of pea gravel or pebbles to the container. This will act as the drainage layer.

2. Layer the gravel or pebbles with a thin layer of charcoal granules to absorb odors, followed by a thin layer of sphagnum moss, which will act as a barrier and prevent the soil from falling into the gravel or pebbles.

3. Layer the moss with ½–1″ (1.5–2.5 cm) of soil (or more if you're using a tall glass container and tall plants).

Add Plants

1. Carefully place the plants into the soil, creating a small hole for the roots and lightly tamping the soil around each plant.

2. Spritz down the inside of the glass with a water mister to remove any extra soil.

3. Add a cork top, if you're using one. This will depend on whether your plants like humidity or not. If you're using a lid, be sure to take it off for a little while every day to let air circulate.

4. Place the terrarium somewhere out of direct sunlight. Now comes the hard part: Leave the terrarium alone. It's a self-contained system, and will do better if not disturbed. Water once a month with spray bottle, or as needed.

I've been giving away planters like these as house-warming gifts ever since I graduated from college and my friends started moving into homes of their own. In retrospect, my first planters were heavy-handed, with every square inch covered in paint. I now prefer to let the natural texture of the planter take center stage. I decorate my markers with alphabet and wildflower stamps.

Decorated Planter & Markers

Pots: 5½" (14 cm) diameter at top,
3½" (9 cm) diameter at bottom, and 7"
(18 cm) high
Markers: 7½" (19 cm) long x 12"
(30.5 cm) wide

MATERIALS

For planters:
Ceramic planter pots with bases
Opaque paint marker in color to
    coordinate with planter
Dish soap
Water
Photocopy paper
Access to a photocopy machine
Graphite transfer paper
Pencil
Scrap paper

For plant markers:
Oven-bake or air-hardening clay
Rolling pin or straight-sided drinking glass
Craft or regular kitchen knife
Alphabet stamps
Decorative stamps
Ink pad (1 or 2 colors)
Sealant, such as Mod Podge or spray
    acrylic sealer (optional)

Decorate Planters

1. Clean the pots with soap and water. Let dry.

2. Photocopy the flower templates above. Place the photocopy on the back side of a piece of transfer paper and place the layered papers in the desired position on a pot. Trace the design on the template with a pencil to transfer the design to the pot. Repeat for the remaining pots.

3. Practice with the paint pen on a scrap of paper to get a sense for the thickness of the marker lines and how quickly the ink flows.

4. When you're comfortable with the marker, trace over the transferred lines on the pot with the paint marker and let dry.

Make Markers

NOTE: If you're using white clay, make sure you're working on a very clean surface. The clay will pick up lint or ink from your hands and the table.

1. Pull off a section of clay about the size of your thumb. Knead it between your palms and fingers until soft and pliable.

2. Roll the clay on your work surface or between your palms to make a snake shape, 6–7″ (15–18 cm) long and ½–¾″ (1.5–2 cm) in diameter.

3. Lightly roll a rolling pin or drinking glass along the length of the clay to flatten it to an even thickness of about ¼″ (6 mm).

4. Gently round one end of the clay. Use a knife to cut the other end into a V-shape.

5. Create a message with the alphabet stamp. Load the stamp with ink and practice stamping on a scrap of paper to figure out how you want to position the stamp on the clay. Load the stamp with ink and press the stamp into the clay.

6. If desired, stamp other images into the clay with decorative stamps.

7. Depending on the clay you're using, bake or air dry according to the manufacturer's instructions.

8. If you want markers to be water-resistant, apply a sealant and let dry.

un prints, or cyanotypes, are made by exposing light-sensitive fabric or paper to sunlight to create an image. In any form, sun prints are magic to me. I think it's the almost underwater, inky look of the blue and the way the white image reveals itself, reminding me of the messages delivered by the Magic 8 ball that my sisters and I played with growing up. Instead of a mysterious message, however, this project broadcasts a decidedly optimistic signal of sunshine and growth.

Sun Print Napkins

FINISHED DIMENSIONS

4 napkins, each measuring 18"
(45.5 cm) square

MATERIALS

1 yard (1 meter) sun print cotton
   (see Resources, page 146)
Flowers, vines, or foliage for making prints
   (see note below)
Thread to match exposed sun print
Iron and ironing board
Clear acrylic grid ruler
Disappearing ink marker
Fabric scissors
Non-UV sheet of glass
Access to a sink with water
Straight pins
Sewing machine

NOTES: Read the instructions and gather
all materials before starting because once
the fabric is exposed to sunlight, you can't
halt process. Iron fabric and cut it into
squares away from any windows or natural
light (or even at night).

Select plant materials by holding them up
to sun and looking at shadow. Select plants
that cast interesting shadows.

When ready to move project outdoors,
transport fabric in its protective cover.
Expose fabric midday when the sun is
strongest. Work on a flat surface, such as
a patio or tabletop.

I place a piece of glass over the top of my
fabric as it's being exposed to keep foliage in
place and prevent wind from blowing it
around. Experiment with a scrap of fabric to
see how long you need to expose your fabric
to make a vivid print. Sun printing cotton
can take anywhere from 10–45 minutes to
fully expose. The warmer and sunnier the
climate, the quicker the exposure time.

Prepare Materials

1. Working away from windows and natural light, remove your fabric from protective black bag and iron out any wrinkles. If you expose the fabric with wrinkles, they may expose into the fabric and leave a permanent mark.

2. Measure the fabric and mark off four 19" (48.5 cm) squares with a disappearing ink marker. Cut out the squares. Keep the fabric flat and away from light until ready to use (see notes on page 101).

3. Take glass, protected fabric, and plant materials outdoors.

Make Sun Prints

1. Working quickly, remove one fabric square from the protective bag and place flat on your work surface. Place the plant materials on top of the fabric as desired and place the glass on top.

2. Expose the fabric to the sun for the time determined on the test sample (see notes on page 101).

3. When the fabric is sufficiently exposed, follow the manufac-turer's instructions for rinsing the fabric with water in a sink until the water runs clear. Let dry.

4. Repeat steps 1–3 for the remaining fabric squares.

Make Napkins

1. Place each fabric square, wrong side up, on an ironing board. Fold over and press ¼" (6 mm) to the wrong side on all edges. Fold over again and press ¼" (6 mm) to the wrong side and pin.

2. Stitch along the inner fold, backstitching at the beginning and end.

Garden Sun Teas

My mom has been making sun tea for as long as I can recall. As a child, I remember her hauling an enormous glass container out of the pantry at the start of every summer and making batch after batch of it. Truth be told, the process doesn't involve much "making" but, instead, setting everything up and getting out of the way so the sun can work its silent magic. My mom would drop several bags of Lipton into the jar, fill with water from the spray-nozzle in our big red kitchen sink, screw the top on, and set it out on our front steps. Even though I wasn't interested in the tea, I always loved watching as the water turned a light sepia and then darkened as the day progressed.

As an adult, I still enjoy watching this solar process. Rather than traditional tea, this is my ritual. Every summer, I take stalks and leaves from my lemon verbena plants, rip the leaves to get the oils to release; and drop them them into a big, 6-cup (1.4 L) Mason jar. Then I fill the jar with water and let the sun do the rest of the work. If I start in the morning, my tea is usually ready by late afternoon.

gather

chapter 3

lways reluctant to throw away my paint chips after settling on a paint color, one day I had the idea to transform them into these postcards. One of the first postcards I made was for my younger sister, Brooke, who was emerging from a long Vermont winter. I used grass green and sky blue colors to put her in a springtime mood. I've also used postcards like these as party invitations. It's a simple way to let people know it's going to be a colorful affair. Just be sure to ask permission before taking extra chips from the paint store.

Paint Chip Postcards

FINISHED DIMENSIONS

4" x 6" (10 x 15 cm)

MATERIALS

2 paint chip sample cards for each postcard
    (see note below)
File folders or light-colored card stock
Decorative stamps (optional)
Vintage-style postage mark stamp
    (optional)
Ink pad
Craft knife
Clear acrylic grid ruler
Self-healing cutting mat
Spray adhesive

NOTE: Choose paint chip sample cards
in colors to reflect a season, mood, or
a color combination you particularly love.
Paint chip sample cards come in different
sizes, and with different numbers of
paint squares. I prefer making one that
is three squares across. You can trim
larger chips to make them smaller or use
as is to make oversized postcards.

Make Postcards

1. Trim the paint chip sample cards to the desired size, if necessary, using a craft knife, ruler, and self-healing cutting mat.
Both sample cards should be trimmed to the same size.

2. Working in a well-ventilated area, apply aerosol adhesive to
one side of the file folder or card stock and the back side of
each paint chip sample card.

3. Lay one paint chip sample card, right side up, on the adhesive
side of the file folder or card stock. Press into place. Position
the second paint chip sample card flush with the first, making
sure the edges are aligned. Press into place. Let dry.

4. Using a ruler and craft knife, trim away excess paper around
the paint chip sample cards to create a postcard.

Decorate Postcards

1. If you're using stamps to decorate the front of the paint chip
postcards, load a stamp with ink and apply the stamp to the
front of the card. Let dry completely in a safe place to prevent
smudging. This may take several hours or overnight because
the surface of the paint chips is coated and not porous. Test
carefully to avoid smudging the ink.

2. If adding a postage mark stamp to the postcard, load a vintage-
style postage mark stamp with ink and stamp the back side of
the postcard along the top edge.

Wildflower Tablecloth

This project is almost like doodling, only on fabric instead of paper, because after you trace and cut the flower and leaf appliqués, you can arrange them in whatever pattern you like—perhaps as shown down the center or clustered organically around the edges. Fusible webbing is ironed onto the appliqués, so they can be adhered easily—no sewing required.

FINISHED DIMENSIONS

54" (137 cm) wide x 96" (244 cm) long

MATERIALS

2½ yards (2½ meters) woven fabric for
    tablecloth (see notes on page 112)
1 yard cotton in contrasting color
    for appliqués
Thread to match fabrics
1 yard (1 meter) paper-backed fusible web
    (see notes on page 112)
Iron and ironing board
Measuring tape
Card stock or other heavy paper
Pencil
Paper scissors
Fabric scissors
Straight pins
Sewing machine
Embroidery needle (optional)
Embroidery floss (optional)

NOTES: Customize the size of the tablecloth to fit your table. Cut the fabric to the dimensions of the tabletop, plus about 17" (43 cm) in each direction to allow for an 8" (20.5 cm) drop on all sides and ¼" (6 mm) double-fold hems. If the tablecloth width needed is greater than the width of the fabric, seam partial widths of fabric to each side of a center panel to achieve the needed width to make the tablecloth. If you vary the tablecloth size from what is shown, adjust the fabric and fusible web yardages accordingly. Customize the appliqué design by mixing different leaf and flower shapes together in a combination that fits your table size.

For this project, you can choose from a wide variety of fusible webs that are available. Just make sure that if you want to add decorative machine stitches, such as a blanket stitch, around the appliqué, you select a web that you can stitch through. Some of the heavier weight fusible webs will gum up your sewing machine if you attempt to sew through them.

Create Appliqué Design

1. Wash, dry, and iron both fabrics. Measure your table and cut the tablecloth fabric to the desired size (see notes at left). Lay the tablecloth fabric on the table or floor to plan the appliqué design layout.

2. Trace the wildflower templates on pages 113–114 onto the paper side of the fusible web, using a pencil. Trace as many wildflower shapes as your project requires (I used 8 large leaves, 10 medium leaves, 5 small leaves, 2 large flowers, 3 tri-leaf flowers, and 2 stamens for my design).

3. Working with an iron and ironing board, fuse the fusible web to the wrong side of the contrasting fabric, following the manufacturer's instructions. Let cool.

4. Cut the wildflower motifs from the fabric with fabric scissors.

5. Peel the paper backing from the wildflower motifs and arrange on the tablecloth fabric until you're satisfied with the design.

6. Press the wildflower motifs onto the tablecloth fabric, following the manufacturer's instructions.

Finish Tablecloth

1. To hem the tablecloth, fold and then press ¼" (6 mm) to the wrong side on all edges. Turn another ¼" (6 mm) to the wrong side, press, and pin in place.

2. Stitch hem in place close to the inner fold.

3. To add embroidery stitches to the appliqués, thread the embroidery needle with embroidery floss and trace the outline of the wildflower motifs, using a running stitch or blanket stitch. You can also stitch around the motifs using a machine blanket stitch, if desired. Follow your sewing machine's user manual to create machine blanket stitches.

wildflower Templates

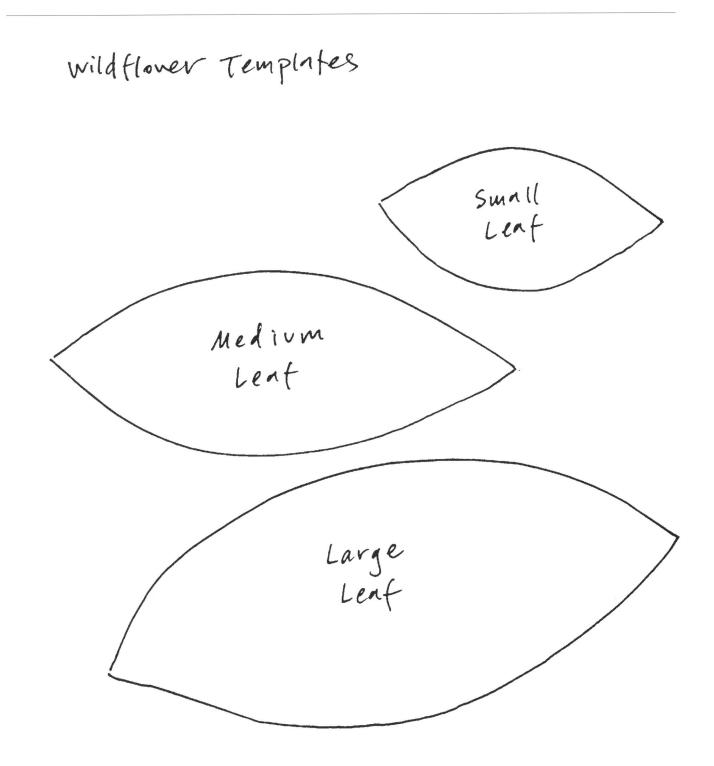

Small Leaf

Medium Leaf

Large Leaf

wildflower templates

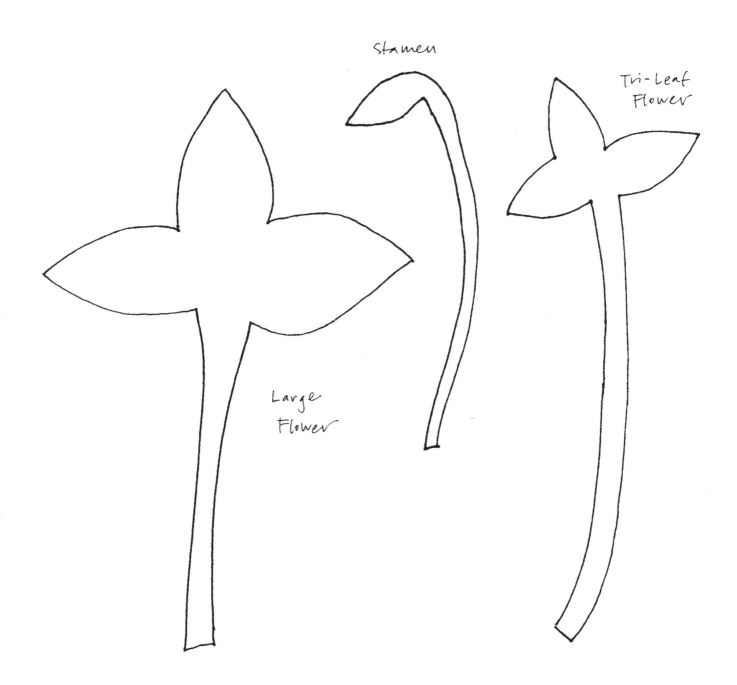

Stamen

Tri-Leaf
Flower

Large
Flower

Farmers' Market Centerpieces

A weekend saunter among tables piled high with fruit at a local farmers' market was the inspiration behind this simple centerpiece. To make one, check out what's fresh and not yet completely ripe at your farmers' market and bring home a small pile of one kind of produce. Arrange your bounty in a simple stand—a cake stand or a wide glass vase or hurricane—and tuck in some snipped herbs or single flowers. Keep the arrangement low enough that you can talk and see over the top, and work within the seasons: whole, unshelled nuts in the winter, bright citrus in the early spring, earthy-colored pears or apples in the fall, and vibrant gem-colored fruit in the summer.

Cloth Picnic Caddy

This pretty case makes transporting utensils and napkins to and from a picnic (or even a backyard barbecue) easy. I recommend oilcloth or vinylized or laminated cotton for this project because these fabrics can be wiped clean with a moist cloth.

FINISHED DIMENSIONS

Closed picnic caddy: 7" (18 cm) wide x
12" (30.5 cm) high
Opened picnic caddy: 12" (30.5 cm) high
x 21" (53.5 cm) wide

MATERIALS

1 yard (1 meter) oilcloth or laminated
    cotton (if using same material for inte-
    rior and exterior), or ½ yard (½ meter)
    each of two contrasting fabrics
3½ yards (3½ meters) cloth ribbon,
    ½" (1.5 cm) wide
Thread to match fabrics
Iron and ironing board
Measuring tape
Sewing scissors or rotary cutter
    and self-healing cutting mat
Disappearing ink fabric marker or
    pencil, depending on fabric choice
Straight pins
Sewing machine with walking foot
    (see note on page 118)

NOTE: There are a lot of choices for this caddy, depending on what expectations you have of your picnic wear. If you want the caddy to be wipeable inside and out, use an oilcloth, vinyl-backed cotton, or even better, one of the new "BPA free" laminated cottons for interior and exterior. If you choose coated fabrics, use a walking foot attachment on your sewing machine, or the fabrics will shift as you sew. I find a zigzag stitch works best. If you don't have a walking foot, you can blanket stitch the fabrics together by hand. On oilcloth or coated fabrics, marks from pins will remain in the fabric after the pins are removed, so try to place pins on the edges of the fabric where the marks will eventually be covered by stitching.

You may use coordinating fabrics for the interior and exterior, or find a fabric with a large scene and use different sections for each piece of the caddy, as I did here.

Cut Fabric and Ribbon

1. Iron the fabrics. Cut a 12" x 21" (30.5 x 53.5 cm) rectangle from both the exterior caddy fabric and the interior caddy fabric, making sure to take into account the orientation of any pattern.

2. Cut one 6" (15 cm) square from fabric for the cutlery pocket.

3. Cut two 4" x 6" (10 x 15 cm) rectangles from fabric for the pockets.

4. Cut four 12" (30.5 cm) lengths of ribbon for the ties.

Add Napkin Ties

1. Position the caddy interior rectangle right side up in landscape orientation on the work surface. Measure and mark three 7″ (18 cm)-wide panels across the width of the fabric, dividing the fabric into even thirds.

2. On the far left panel, mark a point ½″ (1.5 cm) in from the long edges of the panel, 6″ (15 cm) down from the upper edge, using a disappearing ink fabric marker or pencil.

3. Fold one end of each ribbon ½″ (1.5 cm) to the wrong side and press.

4. Center the folded end of one length of ribbon, folded side down, at one of the marked points. Orient the ribbon so the loose end falls toward the center of the panel.

5. Pin in place. Repeat with another ribbon at the remaining marked point.

6. On the sewing machine, edgestitch along the folded edge of the ribbon, backstitching at the beginning; stop with the needle down at the corner, pivot, and continue to stitch along the edge of the ribbon for ½″ (1.5 cm). Stop with the needle down, pivot, and stitch parallel to the folded end of the ribbon. When you reach the edge of the ribbon, stop with the needle down, pivot, and stitch back to the starting point, backstitching at the end to create a stitched square. Stitch an "X" inside the square, backstitching at the beginnings and ends. Repeat the stitched pattern on the remaining ribbon tie.

Add Closure Ties

1. Place the caddy exterior rectangle wrong side up, in landscape orientation. Fold the rectangle vertically in thirds with the left third of the fabric positioned on top, so the folded fabric measures 7″ x 12″(18 x 30.5 cm).

2. Measure 6″ (15 cm) down from the upper edge, along the right edge and in ½″ (1.5 cm). Pin a ribbon, folded side down, to this spot, so the folded edge faces the left edge of the panel.

3. Unfold the caddy and place it right side up, with the ribbon on the right. Measure 8″ (20.5 cm) to the left of the ribbon you just pinned and 6″ (15 cm) down from the upper edge and pin a ribbon to this spot, so its folded edge faces the folded edge of the other exterior ribbon. Re-fold the caddy in thirds, wrong sides in, and make sure the ribbons are correctly placed so they meet when caddy is folded closed.

4. Stitch the ribbons in place using the same method as before.

Add Pocket and Envelopes

1. Pin the 6″ (15 cm) pocket square to the right side of the interior middle panel, centered, ¾″ (2 cm) from the lower edge. Place the 4″ x 6″ (10 x 15 cm) pocket rectangles on the right panel, centering one panel ¾″ (2 cm) from the lower edge and centering the other panel 1″ (2.5 cm) above.

2. Sew all three pocket pieces in place with a zigzag stitch on three sides, leaving the top of each piece open and backstitching at the beginning and end. If you want to create two sections in the middle pocket square, sew a vertical line in the middle of the pocket. This will help keep utensils upright in the pocket.

Assemble Caddy

1. Lay the caddy exterior rectangle on the work surface, wrong side up. Place the caddy interior rectangle on top, so wrong sides are facing. Check the orientation of your patterns and pin in place.

2. Zigzag stitch around all four sides of the caddy, backstitching at the beginning and end.

Foot Pocket Blanket

I came up with this blanket to maximize the amount of time I can spend lounging on the beach or in parks when the fog rolls in and it gets chilly. Modifying an existing blanket—or even cotton shower curtain, in this case—keeps this project simple. Sometimes I use the pocket to keep my feet warm; sometimes to stash books or games; and sometimes I stuff the pocket with extra layers of clothing and use it as a pillow.

You might make your pocket bigger or smaller depending on the size of your blanket. But I find that this size works well for most blankets, and is big enough for two pairs of feet. Fold an approximately 30" (76 cm) square of soft fleece in half. The fold will be the top edge of your pocket. Now turn the other edges under about ½" (1.5 cm) and pin to the front of your blanket, near the bottom. Sew the pocket in place on three sides, leaving the top open.

I made these coasters from bingo cards I saved from a family vacation. Having arrived in North Carolina just in time for a big storm, bodysurfing and beach reading were out. Always resourceful, my dad found a local bingo hall, where my family ended up having a great night playing elbow to elbow with the locals as the rain fell heavy on the metal roof. I saved the cards because I loved the colors, the stamps, and my memories of that rainy night. This project can be made with all sorts of paper memorabilia, such as scorecards from games of hearts, dominos, or euchre, maps, or decorative paper.

Game Night Coasters

FINISHED DIMENSIONS

Each coaster measures 4" (10 cm)
    in diameter

MATERIALS

Set of 4 coasters (either cork or sandstone)
Leftover bingo score cards
Pencil
Paper scissors
Foam brush
Decoupage glue
Craft knife
Self-healing cutting mat

NOTE: If you're using sandstone coasters
with a design, don't use a set with a design
that bleeds all the way to the edge. Find
a set with a design that includes a plain
border around the outer edges.

Make Coasters

1. Place a coaster upside down on top of a bingo card, positioning the coaster so it covers the part of the card you want to use.

2. Using a pencil, lightly trace around the coaster. Cut just inside the marked line.

3. Place the cut-out on top of a coaster, right side up, to make sure it fits. Trim if necessary.

4. Using a foam brush, apply a thin layer of decoupage glue to the top of the coaster. Place the score card cut-out on top.

5. Smooth the score card cut-out over the coaster; work from the center and use your fingers and the heel of your hand to gently press out any wrinkles or air bubbles.

6. Repeat steps 1–5 to make additional coasters.

Trim and Finish

1. Let the coasters dry, checking occasionally to see if you need to press out any air bubbles that may have crept in. Check to be sure the edges of the paper don't hang over the edges of the coasters. If they do, turn the coasters upside down on a self-healing cutting mat, and then carefully run a sharp craft knife along the edges to trim the excess paper. Be sure to do this when the paper is completely dry, or the knife will tug the wet paper instead of cut it.

2. When the coasters are dry, apply a coat of decoupage glue to the top of each to make the surfaces waterproof.

Game Night Poetry

I grew up in a rip-roaring, game-playing family, where we spent reunions playing fierce rounds of the drawing or the dictionary game (precursors to Pictionary and Fictionary) as well as rummy, dominoes, and cribbage. These are still family classics, but in recent years, we've added a new one called the Poetry Game.

The idea is to create collectively written "poems" by taking turns writing each line. Start with as many pieces of paper as there are people and ask everyone to write "1, 3, 5, 3, 1" in a vertical column down the left side of their paper. Those numbers tell you how many words will be in that particular line of the poem. So everyone starts by writing one word, and passing the paper to the right. Next, everyone writes three words and passes again, and so on, until you've finished the poems.

But here's the kicker: You should only see the last line written when you're adding your own word or phrase. So after you write your line, fold the paper so the person you pass to can only see the line you just wrote. Sometimes this results in ludicrous, nonsensical poems. But more often than not, a trippy sort of mind-share happens around the table, and the poem goes in directions you never would have imagined if you read all the lines preceding yours.

As with most games, this one may sound tame. But gather a group of imaginative people, give it a couple rounds, and you'll soon see how quickly the atmosphere and topics turn wildly creative and unpredictable.

Starry Night Garlands

When I first aimed a can of metallic silver spray paint at the ubiquitous Styrofoam balls I picked up at my local craft shop, I had no idea what the result would be. But it turns out that a thorough coat of this shimmery paint transforms these mundane orbs into cool party decorations. Take several strands and hang in loose swags on a wall or hang a simple string over a door.

FINISHED DIMENSIONS

Length varies
Decorative elements measure
1½"–4" (4–10 cm) wide

MATERIALS

For all garland versions:
Styrofoam balls in two different sizes
      (I used 1" [2.5 cm] and 1½"
      [4 cm] balls)
Silver aerosol paint
Old cardboard box
Tapestry needle

For plain ribbon version:
1 spool sheer ombre ribbon, ½"
(1.5 cm) wide

For version with flat paper flowers:
Card stock in desired colors
Flower-shaped craft punch
Embroidery floss

For flower bomb version:
Tissue paper in desired colors
Silver cording
Paper scissors
Ruler
Pencil

Prepare Styrofoam Balls
(for all garland versions)

Place the Styrofoam balls in a cardboard box. Working outside or in a well-ventilated area, paint the balls with silver spray paint, shaking the box to ensure the balls are completely painted. Let the Styrofoam balls dry, shaking the box occasionally to prevent them from sticking together. Apply another coat of paint in the same manner, if necessary, and let dry completely.

Make Plain Ribbon Garland

NOTE: Because the Styrofoam balls are tightly secured to the ribbon, you can hang the garland horizontally or vertically.

1. Thread ribbon through the tapestry needle, but don't cut ribbon off the spool. This will allow you to create a garland as long as the ribbon on the spool.

2. Pass the needle through the Styrofoam balls, one at a time, alternating randomly between the two sizes of balls, and varying the amount of ribbon you leave between the balls. Be sure to leave long ribbon tails at the ends for hanging. Continue until you reach the desired length of garland and cut ribbons.

Make Garland with Flat Paper Flowers

1. Cut out as many paper flowers as desired, using different colors of card stock and a flower-shaped craft punch.

2. Thread embroidery floss through the tapestry needle. Leave floss in a bundle so you can create as long a garland as you want.

3. Alternate passing the needle through different-sized Styrofoam balls and paper flowers. Continue until you reach the desired length of the garland, leaving long floss tails at the ends for hanging, and then trim the excess floss.

Make Flower Bomb Garland

1. For each flower bomb, cut 6 layers of tissue paper, each 3½" x 4" (9 x 10 cm).

2. For each flower bomb, layer two 3½" x 4" (9 x 10 cm) pieces of tissue, and then fold the tissue back and forth, in ½" (1.5 cm)-wide folds, accordion-style, along one long edge, until you reach the opposite side. Repeat two more times using two pieces of tissue paper each time, so you have three pleated lengths of 2-ply tissue paper for each flower bomb.

3. To assemble the garland, thread the tapestry needle with silver cording.

4. Pass the needle through one or more Styrofoam balls, varying the sizes of the balls. When you want to add a flower bomb, make a knot in the cording where you want the flower to be. Push the needle through the center of each of three pleated lengths of the tissue paper. When all three lengths have been added, make another knot on other side of the tissue paper, close to the paper to keep the flower center in place.

5. Turn the lengths of paper so two folded lengths make an "X" with the last folded length bisecting the "X." To create flowers, carefully pull open all six pieces of tissue paper. First fan the accordion folds open, then gently pull each layer of tissue paper apart and away from each other to make a round ball shape. Be careful to keep the bisected "X" arrangement so the flower will be a full, round sphere.

6. Once all layers are open, gently scrunch the paper if needed to even all layers of tissue into a round flower.

7. Repeat steps 4–6 as many times as needed to create a garland as long as you desire. Leave long tails at the ends for hanging and trim the excess cording. Knot the cord at the ends to prevent fraying.

Top and bottom: Flower Bomb Garland
Center: Garland with Flat Paper Flowers
NOTE: Plain Ribbon Garland is shown on pages 126–127.

For this project, I transformed a silkscreened tea towel into an apron. Starting with a tea towel rather than yardage saves time because the side and bottom edges are finished before you start. Although it's tempting to put away items like this for special occasions, I urge you to use this apron often, as it gets better and better as it wears and softens.

Tea
Towel
Apron

FINISHED DIMENSIONS

15" (38 cm) long x 17" (43 cm) wide, not
including ribbon tie

MATERIALS

Tea towel
3–4 yards (3–4 meters) ribbon, 1½"
    (4 cm) wide
Thread to match towel
Full-length mirror to check length of
    towel when held up to your waist
Iron and ironing board
Clear acrylic grid ruler
Chalk pencil
Fabric scissors
Straight pins
Sewing machine
Large safety pin

Make Apron

1. Hold one long edge of the tea towel up to your waist and check the appearance in a mirror. The length should be at least 2″ (5 cm) longer than the desired finished length to allow for the casing at the top (assuming you're using 1½″ (4 cm) wide ribbon as I did). If the tea towel is too short, look for a longer tea towel.

2. To determine the length of the apron, stand in front of the mirror and fold the upper long edge of the tea towel to the back side until you are satisfied with the length. You must fold at least 2″ (5 cm) to the back side to allow for the casing. Holding the fold in place, remove the tea towel.

3. Press the fold at the upper edge of the tea towel, making sure the fold is straight.

4. Measure down from the fold on the back side, the width of the ribbon plus ½″ (1.5 cm) and mark a chalk line parallel to the fold. Trim on the marked line.

5. Fold and then press ⅜″ (1 cm) to the wrong side along the trimmed edge. Then refold on the two crease lines to make the casing for the ribbon. Pin the casing in place.

6. Edgestitch along the inner fold to create a channel for the ribbon.

7. Attach the safety pin to the end of the ribbon and insert the safety pin into the channel. Pass the safety pin with the ribbon through the channel and pull on the ribbon until the amount of ribbon on each side of the apron is equal.

8. Try on the apron and decide how long to make the ribbon ties. I like to have enough ribbon to wrap around my back and tie at the front. If your ribbon is too long, mark where you want the ribbon to end, and trim ½″ (1.5 cm) beyond the mark (I used a 96″ (244 cm) length of ribbon).

9. At each end of the ribbon, fold over and press ¼″ (6 mm) to the wrong side twice. Stitch along the edge of the inner fold at each ribbon end.

Flea Market Place Settings

I have a deep love of pattern. It can be a singular pattern set against a plain background, or a small little riot of different patterns, like cushions on a couch or a contrasting skirt and top. I admit that trotting out a couple different patterns in public can provoke odd looks or questions, but it's pretty low-risk to test how patterns work alongside each other in the privacy of your own dining room or kitchen.

I regularly scour flea markets and kitchen department sales for patterned plates, and have amassed a cheery stack. And while I know the plates I snap up are meant to appear in groupings of the same pattern, I tend to buy one piece of each. I consider it my small colorful rebellion against the typically monochromatic dining room table.

Stitched Photo Tapestry

There are few things more treasured than old family photographs that capture the big and small moments of well-lived lives. For this project, I stitched together worn photos and postcards, and then mounted the project on foam core. If you can't bear to sew original photographs, you can make digital replicas on photo paper for the same effect.

FINISHED DIMENSIONS

This arrangement measures 12" x 24"
(30.5 x 61 cm) at longest and widest points

MATERIALS

Old photos and postcards (see note below)
Painter's tape
Sewing machine
Thread
Piece of foam core, as large as the
　　finished photo collage
Pencil
Craft knife
Canned goods or other objects to
　　weight down photo collage
Cutting board or self-healing cutting mat
Ruler
Craft knife
Spray adhesive
Sawtooth hanger or adhesive
　　picture hanger

NOTE: If you don't want to use old photos
for this project, you can scan photos into
a computer and print them onto photo
paper. You can also use paper scissors with
deckle edges to cut out the photos to mimic
the irregular edges of vintage photos.

Assemble Photo Collage

1. Lay the photos and postcards on a table or flat surface. Arrange the photos and postcards with edges touching into a pleasing arrangement. For variety, place some images horizontally and others vertically and use postcards throughout the arrangement.

2. When you're satisfied with your layout, tape adjacent photos to each other with painter's tape to temporarily secure their placement.

3. To stitch photos together, it's easiest to work with small groupings. Overlap the edges of two adjacent photos and stitch together using a machine zigzag stitch, backstitching at the beginning and end. Join an additional photo to the pair in the same manner to make a small grouping. Stitch the remaining photo into groupings, then sew the groupings to each other, until all photos are joined.

Mount Collage

1. Lay the photo collage on top of a piece of foam core and lightly trace around the edges with a pencil. I find it helps to place canned goods on top of the photo collage, to keep it in place. As you pencil around the images, use your hand to press the photos flat so you have as precise an outline as possible.

2. Place the foam core on a cutting board or self-healing cutting mat. Cut just inside the marked pencil line, using a ruler and craft knife.

3. Working in a well-ventilated area, spray the top of the foam core and the back side of the stitched photo collage with spray adhesive.

4. Press the photo collage into place on top of the foam core. Let dry.

5. Add a sawtooth hanger or an adhesive picture hanger to the back of the foam core and hang the collage.

3/9/37

Glacier National Park

POST CARD

U.S. POSTAGE

2

MINNEAPOLIS MINN
JUL 24
11:30 AM
1914

Mrs Claude Ellis,
Sprangville
New York.

Just returning from
a beautiful trip. The
East is fine and quite
primitive. I hope
everyone especially
John Rus is

"Visit Glacier National Park"
Where Glaciers of the long ago
lay gleaming 'neath eternal snow.

GREAT
NORTHERN
RAILWAY

Dotty Felt Placemats & Table Runner

Rather than using a full tablecloth, sometimes I like to dress up our wooden dining room table with placemats and a table runner. I love the play of positive and negative space in this set; the circular cutouts through which you can see the tabletop remind me of portholes in a ship.

Felt doesn't fray, so you don't have to finish the edges on this project. But I find that hand or machine-stitching around the cutouts in a contrasting color adds sophistication.

FINISHED DIMENSIONS

Placemats: 12" (30.5 cm) long x 17"
(43 cm) wide
Table runner: 12" (30.5 cm) long x 54"
(137 cm) long

MATERIALS

(for a set of four placemats and one table
runner)
1¼ yards (1¼ meters) wool felt, at
    least 54" (137 cm) wide
Thread to match or contrast with felt,
    depending on preference
Three small objects with circle shapes in
    different sizes, such as a jar lid, small
    drinking glasses, or spools of thread
Chalk pencil or water-soluble fabric marker
Fabric scissors
Sewing machine
Iron and ironing board

Cut Placemats and Runner

NOTE: Very sharp fabric scissors make these precise edges possible. Since felt doesn't fray, the edges can be left raw. That means they need to be cut with smooth, clean lines. Accomplish this by making long, even cuts with your scissors.

1. From wool felt, cut four rectangles, 12″ x 17″ (30.5 x 43 cm), for the placemats and one rectangle, 12″ x 54″(30.5 x 137 cm), for the table runner.

2. To round the corners of the placemats and table runner, place the lid of a jar or a drinking glass at a corner so the curve meets the straight side edges. Trace the curve with a chalk pencil or a water-soluble marker and cut rounded corners with sharp scissors. Repeat at the remaining corners.

3. To decide where to create circle cutouts, place objects with circular shapes near the edges of the placemats and table runner until you're satisfied with the placement of the circles (refer to the project photos for suggested placement).

4. If you are using a dark color of felt, trace around the circle shapes with a chalk pencil to transfer the circles to the felt. For light colors of felt, trace with a water-soluble marker.

5. Cut the circles out with fabric scissors, cutting just outside the marked lines. You can be less precise with these circles than you were with the rounded outer corners, since these edges will be encased in zigzag stitches.

6. Repeat steps 3–5 to add additional circles to the remaining placemats and table runner. Try changing the arrangement of the circles on each placemat and the runner, for a less matchy-matchy look.

Finish Cutout

1. Set your sewing machine to a zigzag stitch and sew around the inside of each circle, backstitching at the beginning and end.

2. If the sewing made the felt a little wavy, press the felt flat again with a warm iron set to the wool setting.

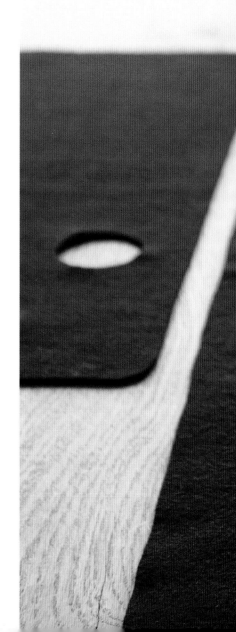

One day while milling around in the aisles of my favorite neighborhood hardware store, inspiration struck and I decided to see if I could use concrete to create pretty trivets. As anyone who has ever scratched their name in a wet sidewalk knows, concrete takes on the impression of anything pressed into it beautifully. My trivets, embedded with branch patterns that remind me of bare trees in late winter, have a beautiful not-quite-smooth, not-quite-rough surface texture. Of course, they also do a great job of protecting tabletops.

Winter Marsh Trivet

FINISHED DIMENSIONS

7½" (19 cm) diameter as shown but
can vary depending on size of saucer used
as mold

MATERIALS

4 pounds (1.8 kg) cement, or cement
    stepping stone kit (available in kids
    section of craft stores), to make 2 trivets
Water
Cement tint, if you want to color your trivet
    (see notes on page 144)
Canola or vegetable oil
2 round 7–8" (18–20.5 cm) plastic plant
    saucers, for molds
Dried or artificial branches or decorative
    items to make an impression in or
    embed in the cement (see notes on
    page 144)
Plastic mixing bucket, at least
    2½ quarts (3.8 L) capacity
Liquid ingredient measuring cup
Tablespoon (measuring spoon), if adding
    cement tint
Mixing stick
Paper towels
Tweezers
12" (30.5 cm) felt square for each
    trivet backing
Chalk pencil or pen
Fabric scissors
Hot glue gun and glue sticks

NOTES: You can find cement tints at well-stocked hardware stores, where you can also buy cement, but possibly not in small amounts. Many craft stores stock small amounts of cement packaged as a stepping stone kit. Four pounds of cement will make approximately two 7½" (19 cm) trivets. If using a cement tint, follow the manufacturer's instructions and add the tint to the water before adding cement mix. Tints are very concentrated so you should only need a tablespoon or so of tint to color the cement. Use more to achieve deep colors.

If you're adding an impression to your trivet with twigs or branches, look for items that are thick enough to leave an impression in the cement. Delicate flowers will not make a vivid impression in the cement. If you plan to leave items embedded in the cement, be sure to use items that can tolerate heat, as hot pans will be placed on the trivet.

Make Trivets

1. If working with a cement stepping stone kit, mix the water and cement according to the manufacturer's instructions and add cement tint, if using (see notes above). The mixture should be the consistency of a thick milkshake. Make sure the mixture is stirred well. If you are not using a kit, pour about 1⅓ cups (315.5 mL) of water into a bucket and stir in cement tint, if using. Add 4 pounds (1.8 kg) of cement in thirds, mixing each addition thoroughly before continuing.

2. Use a paper towel to apply a thin layer of oil to the inside of the plastic molds.

3. Pour cement into the molds to a depth of at least 1" (2.5 cm).

4. Lift filled molds and "drop" onto a flat surface from a height of a few inches to evenly distribute the cement and release air bubbles.

Embellish Trivet

1. Let the cement set for 15–30 minutes before adding embellishments. Depending on the temperature and consistency of your cement, it may take longer for the cement to set enough to hold embellishments or embedded objects. When the cement has started to set, press a branch or decorative item into the still-wet cement. Leave for about a minute.

2. To create the impression, remove the branch or decorative item from the cement with a tweezers, being careful to lift the item straight up—don't drag it across the surface. If you mess up the design, just smooth over the design and try again. Cement is more forgiving than you might imagine. You may also want to leave objects permanently embedded in the cement.

3. If water pools into the impression after you remove the branch or decorative object, fold a paper towel and carefully blot excess water with the edge of the towel. Let the cement dry completely. This takes 24–48 hours.

Finish Trivets

1. Remove the cement trivets from the molds.

2. Lay the trivets on top of the felt squares and trace around the outer edge with a chalk pencil or a pen. Cut just inside the marked line with fabric scissors.

3. Apply hot glue to the underside of the trivet and press the felt into place.

resources

The tools and materials used in the projects in this book are generally available at craft, fabric, and art supply stores nationwide. Following is a list of sources for some specialty supplies that may not be stocked everywhere.

Bee Culture
www.beeculture.com
Links to local beekeeping groups

Bee Source
www.beesource.com
General beekeeping resources

Best Containers
www.bestcontainers.com
Flat, round tins

Blue Sunprints
www.bluesunprints.com
Sun print cotton

Feather Pads
www.featherstore.com
Feather pad for Feathered Headband

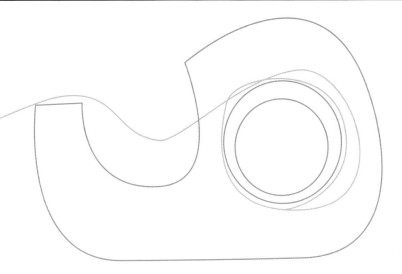

Glasshouse Works
www.glasshouseworks.com
Plants for terrariums

Hambly Screen Prints
www.hamblyscreenprints.com
Rub-on transfers

Happy Tape
www.happytape.com
Japanese washi tape

Mountain Rose Herbs
www.mountainroseherbs.com
Bulk herbs and essential oils

Paper Source
www.paper-source.com
Decorative paper, stamps, art supplies

Plaid
www.plaidonline.com
Hard Coat Mod Podge

Purl Soho
www.purlsoho.com
Wool felt and laminated fabric

The Scarlet Sage Herb Co.
www.scarletsageherb.com
Bulk herbs, herb books, essential oils

Super Buzzy
www.superbuzzy.com
Laminated fabric

Acknowledgments

When I decided I wanted to write a book, I didn't know where to send the proposal. So I spent a couple of long afternoons in local bookstores, crouched in the craft aisle, looking for books that were beautiful, well written, and well produced. When I found them, most of the spines read STC Craft/Melanie Falick Books. And in their acknowledgments, authors expressed gratitude to Melanie for her vision and care. So I packaged up my proposal and sent it to Melanie. A few weeks later she called me, and now I get to do the same here. Melanie generously allowed me the time to grow my ideas and helped me distill them into this book. For that, I am grateful and proud.

Thanks to Thayer Allyson Gowdy for her gorgeous photographs and Karen Schaupeter for creating beautiful settings. The atmosphere you created in these projects is exactly what I was looking for—and more. And to Lisa Wong Jackson and her family, thank you for letting us invade your lovely home for a day.

Thanks to onethread for their inspired design and layouts. All the choices you made brought out the very best in the projects.

Thanks to Dawn Anderson for her meticulous eye for detail and accuracy.

I'm grateful to my colleagues and friends at KQED, for keeping me part of the family even when it seemed ludicrous that I was turning down reporting work to sew at my dining room table. Thank you for the flexibility and support.

Thanks to Liz Seymour and Angie Wu at the *Washington Post,* who give me the opportunity to dream up monthly craft projects under their sharp and thoughtful editorship.

Thanks to Sarah Sockit Moseley, who was patient and wonderful and a believer from our first conversation.

Thanks to everyone who cheered me along and had ideas for a book party even before I had a publisher. I am wildly fortunate to call so many big-hearted people my friends. In particular, Heather Ross buoyed me up over pondside rosé and long-distance phone calls. And Sarah Flotard offered brainstorming, love, and support over slow-cooked meals and cocktails.

Thanks to my family—my small army of cousins, aunts, uncles, and in-laws—who always rooted for me. My niece and nephew, Ada and Owen, helped in every way they could, allowing me to raid their rooms and then gamely jumping in for the photo shoot. To my sisters, Robyn and Brooke, I still have your ecstatic messages and photos from the day this proposal was accepted. Your love and support never flagged. You make me proud to be a member of the Wilkinson sisters trio. And to my parents, who set the original example of turning sometimes-crazy ideas into reality, thank you for your conviction and encouragement in everything I do—this book is only the most recent example.

Mostly, thanks to my husband, Mike, for your fierce belief in me. I feel the same way about you.

Index of Projects & Ideas